D1706726

DATE DUE

NUMBER TWENTY-ONE
The Walter Prescott Webb Memorial Lectures

Essays on the
History of North American Discovery
and Exploration

[THE WALTER PRESCOTT WEBB MEMORIAL LECTURES]

Essays on the History of North American Discovery and Exploration

BY DAVID B. QUINN, ROBERT H. FUSON,
OLIVE PATRICIA DICKASON, CORNELIUS J. JAENEN,
ELIZABETH A. H. JOHN, WILLIAM H. GOETZMANN

Introduction by HOWARD R. LAMAR
Edited by STANLEY H. PALMER
and DENNIS REINHARTZ

Published for the University of Texas at Arlington by
Texas A&M University Press: College Station

The paper used in this book meets the minimum requirements of the American National Standard for Permanence of Paper for Printed Library Materials, Z39.48-1984. Binding materials have been chosen for durability.

Library of Congress Cataloging-in-Publication Data

Essays on the history of North American discovery and
  exploration.
    (The Walter Prescott Webb memorial lectures ; no. 21)
    1. America—Discovery and exploration. 2. North Ameri-
ca—Description and travel. I. Palmer, Stanley H.
II. Reinhartz, Dennis. III. Title. IV. Series:
Walter Prescott Webb memorial lectures ; 21.
E121.E87 1988   970.01   87-10166
ISBN 0-89096-373-8 (alk. paper)

Manufactured in the United States of America
FIRST EDITION

To Jenkins and Virginia Garrett

Contents

Preface

Discovery, that is, the documented (e.g., on a map) initial contact with the unknown, and exploration, the understanding of discovery, have together constituted a heroic dimension of the human saga from its very beginnings. The first recorded expedition was sponsored by Queen Hatshepsut, Bronze Age Egypt's only female pharaoh, to Punt (Somalia) for the purpose of trade in the middle of the fifteenth century B.C. Data on the latest expeditions, launched into space by the Soviet Union and the United States, appear in daily newspapers and news broadcasts. From Yuri Gagarin, the first human in space, through the space shuttle *Challenger*, these new missions of discovery and exploration have continued to expand humanity's horizons and point the way to the future.

The story of discovery and exploration, especially of North America, contributes significantly to what Walter Prescott Webb called the "high adventure" of history. It is therefore quite appropriate that the theme selected for the twenty-first annual Walter Prescott Webb Memorial Lectures, presented at the University of Texas at Arlington on March 12–13, 1986, was North American discovery and exploration.

In the first essay David B. Quinn, emeritus professor at the University of Liverpool and a past president of the prestigious Hakluyt Society, considers the initial European colonization of North America and carefully differentiates the Spanish, French, and English experiences. As Professor Quinn indicates in his conclusion, his topic is but an opening chapter in the history of the European penetration of North America. It is fitting that his essay begins this volume.

Robert H. Fuson, emeritus professor of geography at the University of South Florida, is the winner of the 1986 Webb-Smith essay competition. The award is offered each year for the best essay submitted on the theme of the Lectures and is funded by the same generous endowment from C. B. Smith of Austin that also helps support the Webb Lecture series. Professor Fuson's essay brings together what is known about John Cabot, and it usefully separates fact from myth. In so doing, Fuson probes the background of the controversy surrounding this early North American explorer.

In her essay, Olive Patricia Dickason, professor of history at the University of Alberta, examines the development of related Old World legal concepts with regard to sovereignty and their application to the New World during the first great era of exploration and colonization. Professor Dickason also shows how these concepts were transformed by the New World rivalries of the European powers and by the New World environment.

The essay by Cornelius J. Jaenen, professor of history at the University of Ottawa, was not a part of the Webb Lectures. It is based on the keynote address made by Professor Jaenen at a monthlong program, "The Sun King: Louis XIV—Texas and the French Experience," sponsored in part by the UT–Arlington Department of History in April, 1986. After hearing Professor Jaenen's paper, the editors thought it perfect for inclusion in this volume and prevailed upon him to submit this essay. Jaenen provides an incisive analysis of the uniqueness of the French contact with the native peoples of New France, with special emphasis on the experiences of the eighteenth century.

The history of discovery and the history of cartography are intimately interwoven. In her essay, Elizabeth A. H. John of Austin introduces the shadowy figure of Juan Pedro Walker, cartographer of the early nineteenth-century trans-Mississippi frontier and Texas. She adeptly uses Walker to reconstruct this little-known phase of North American mapping and to illustrate the connection between cartography and discovery.

The concluding essay in this volume is a brief piece by William H. Goetzmann, the Pulitzer Prize–winning Dickson, Allen & Anderson Centennial Professor in American Studies and History at the University of Texas at Austin. Professor Goetzmann discusses the transfer of images of the frontier, recorded in the explorers' paintings and drawings sent back to the people in the American East and in Europe during the nineteenth century.

The occasion of the 1986 Webb Memorial Lectures also marked the tenth anniversary of the generous donation of manuscripts, maps and other graphics, rare books, newspapers, and microfilm dealing with the history of Texas and the Greater Southwest, by Jenkins and Virginia Garrett of Fort Worth to the Library of the University of Texas at Arlington. Garrett, a Webb student, a prominent attorney, and a former University of Texas System regent, and his wife are longtime staunch advocates and benefactors of the University of Texas at Arlington. Their gift has become the core of the Division of Special Collections—the Jenkins Garrett Library and the Cartographic History Library—housed in specially designed quarters on the sixth floor of the University Library. Among its holdings, the Garrett Library contains the nation's most comprehensive collection on the Mexican War of 1846–48; the Cartographic History Library is a center for the study of the exploration and mapping of the New World, with emphasis on Texas and the Gulf of Mexico.

The Garretts were honored by the Department of History at a special dinner on the evening of March 12, 1986, and were presented with a lifetime membership in the Society for the History of Discoveries. It is with heartfelt thanks and in recognition of their continuing generosity and support that this volume is dedicated to Jenkins and Virginia Garrett.

Stanley H. Palmer
Dennis Reinhartz

Essays on the
History of North American Discovery
and Exploration

Introduction

ONE of the most enduring contributions of Walter Prescott Webb's *The Great Frontier* was to demonstrate the dramatic economic and political impact of the New World of the Americas on the Old World of Europe. By stressing the American contribution, he forced historians to think in terms of reciprocal impact. That approach now seems so obvious and logical that it hardly seems new. Yet only a few years ago Alfred Crosby's *The Columbian Exchange* made news when it expanded the concept of intercontinental reciprocity to include biological and ecological exchanges between the Old World and the New. In 1986, Donald W. Meinig expanded the idea of a tricontinental set of exchanges between Africa, Europe, and the Americas in his seminal study, *Atlantic America, 1492–1800.*

The latest volume in the published series of the Walter Prescott Webb Memorial Lectures, which are held each spring on the campus of the University of Texas at Arlington, focuses on the history of North American discovery, and thus continues the Webbian theme of interaction between Europe and America, but in a number of fresh and arresting ways. As readers will see, the six distinguished historians of exploration whose essays are presented here have not only treated the subject of their particular area of the vast topic of North American discovery but also suggested new perspectives. And these authors have found, though often in very different fields, common and recurring themes that give an added coherence to the history of North American exploration and discovery.

The writers discuss, among many other things, the New World as seen by European canonical and civil legalists, by the explorers themselves, such as Cabot and Verrazzano, and by their historical interpreters. There follows a remarkably fresh essay on the early French contact with the Amerindian societies of North America in which the larger meaning of these societies for Europeans is treated. Finally, two essays explain how a coherent image of the New World was created by mapmakers, land explorers, scientists, and artists. Using a broad-

ranging interdisciplinary approach, an understandably appropriate
attitude for historians of exploration, the authors have embraced in
their essays the fields of comparative, intellectual, legal, and social
history, as well as the disciplines of art history, anthropology, ethnol-
ogy, and geography. Taken together these essays constitute an impressive early volume in what will undoubtedly be a spate of studies that
will commemorate the forthcoming five-hundredth anniversary of Columbus's discovery of America in 1492.

The first accounts of the European discovery of the Americas are
interesting, even mesmerizing, as they undoubtedly were before Webb
wrote *The Great Frontier*, and presumably will be as long as historians ply their craft. Even the most factual and even-paced survey texts
take on a tone of expectation and excitement when they describe Columbus's first voyage, recount Cortez's conquest of the Aztec empire
in Mexico, or follow Cabeza de Vaca's despairing but historic journey
from Florida across the South and Southwest to the northern provinces of New Spain. With a similar sense of excitement students still
respond to the grand chronicle of the coming of Spain, France, and
England to North America. They associate Spain with conquest of vast
stretches of land and millions of Indians and with gold and missions;
France with Canada, the Mississippi valley, and the fur trade; and
England with Atlantic coast colonization, settlements expanding westward, and brutal wars with the Indians.

Although future scholarship is not likely to change these stereo-
typical short-cut descriptions of the endeavors of these three nation-
states in the New World, we have passed from an age of grand narrative to more analytical accounts, a change accompanied by a virtual
explosion of knowledge—and interest—about native societies, a new
appreciation of the American environment and the often disastrous
European impact on it, and inevitably, from those two awarenesses,
to a new perspective on the old facts and sometimes even a total new
meaning for these facts.

Happily the six essays all demonstrate these new approaches and
interests. In "Colonies in the Beginning: Examples from North America," David B. Quinn, professor emeritus of modern history, University of Liverpool, and author of books on the Roanoke voyages, early
voyages to New England, and early French settlement, continues the
theme of revision of older views. Noting that we must start our study
of North American colonial history before 1607 or 1620, he urges historians to study the pre- and protosettlement period before 1625. If
one looks at the early Spanish experience in the New World, for exam-

ple, it seems less and less that the Spanish empire was born out of the experiences of the *reconquista*. Rather, the Spanish system in the New World had its ups and downs depending on the monarch's interest and what was happening at home. Although Spain did invent a New World government from a distance, it was so obsessed with paper, Quinn believes, that it was less effective than it might have been.

In the case of France, Professor Quinn finds that the older image of its government as fostering New World exploration and settlement falls before the evidence that French port towns took the initiative in developing New France. Even in the later period France was not so concerned with bureaucracy as it was "affected by what pressures important merchant groups could bring on the government."

Quinn points out that from 1630 onward, England was "the first effective North American colonizing power," but here again it appears that in the early period the English let the colonists do things on their own.

Quinn's essay poses several arresting questions. Is our account of the role and impact of powerful European nation-states exaggerated? Should the focus be on events in the colonies? Is there evidence that more "freedom" in terms of absence of control existed on all three frontiers? All in all, he provides a splendid example of how we must pay close attention to the facts about a period and not let what seem to be overriding precedents or retrospective generalizations cloud our view.

Robert Fuson, emeritus professor of geography at the University of South Florida, has written a delightful and intriguing essay, "The John Cabot Mystique," which reminds us of the frequent difficulty encountered in getting at the actual facts of New World discovery. "The John Cabot Mystique" resembles a research and historiographical spy thriller about John Cabot, discoverer of Newfoundland for England, and his ambitious, deceitful son Sebastian, who Professor Fuson believed tried to appropriate his father's accomplishments as his own.

Fuson provides a splendid case study of how scholars and non-scholars have taken insufficient evidence to make Cabot the so-called true discoverer of Florida as well as of Canada. Fuson smashes these claims in a brilliant argument and concludes that Cabot did not make history, "he was created by history." Scholars, he finds, are guilty of immortalizing one "of the most obscure navigators of the fifteenth century" because of "national, provincial, and personal biases."

The essay by Olive Patricia Dickason, professor of history at the

University of Alberta, analyzes the European legal and religious mindset both before and after 1492. In her "Old World Law, New World Peoples, and Concepts of Sovereignty," Professor Dickason finds that European canonists and civilists had been debating the status of non-Christian peoples since the twelfth and thirteenth centuries. While some churchmen argued that non-Christians had a right to their own property and their own governments, others claimed that they had no legitimate authority outside the church. If infidels refused to recognize and obey the power and authority of the Roman church, then they "are not fit to have kingdoms, governments, jurisdiction nor dominion."

One sees at once how the European legal mindset would not only extend the debate to New World peoples but open the way for different countries to argue their particular cases. As Dickason notes, the Spanish used papal spiritual authority but did not allow papal political authority over their American holdings. The latecomer French, finding that all lands were claimed by Spain and Portugal, found it convenient to assert the principles of freedom of trade and freedom of the seas as a way of gaining right of access. In trying to justify their invasion of Portuguese Brazil to trade for dyestuffs, they allied with the native Tupi and said that the Tupi, being the original inhabitants, had a right to live there. As Dickason points out, the French later used this argument to justify their claim of the Saint Lawrence region.

Dickason traces the legal debate over the status of New World peoples and the concept of sovereignty down to the Nootka Sound crisis of 1790, when the British made the first successful challenge to the Spanish claim of sovereignty on grounds of the doctrine of occupation. It is no wonder that Thomas Jefferson followed the Nootka crisis closely, for its precedent-setting outcome operated to the benefit of the United States as its population expanded westward into disputed lands. All in all, Dickason's essay gives an invaluable coherence to European behavior in America over time.

One of the most rewarding recent fields of study relating to the age of North American settlement has been the interaction between Indians and Europeans. Whether it has been at the level of biological and ecological swapping as treated in Alfred Crosby's *The Columbian Exchange,* or the economic and ecological impact as described by William Cronon in his *Changes in the Land,* the result has been that Indians have been restored to a more dynamic role in the shaping of early North American history. Building on his own previous works in Indian-white relations, Cornelius Jaenen, professor of history at the University of Ottawa, makes a signal contribution with his essay, "Characteristics of French-Amerindian Contact in New France." Jaenen believes that French and Indian relations in Canada were unique because the authorities at Quebec were paternalistic rather than arbitrary. The French did not displace populations, and they saw native self-government as an instrument of French power. The French also never quite asserted sovereignty. While they claimed the land, they did not claim the people. And even when they lost Canada to the British in 1763, they told the Indians that they had ceded French rights in Canada but not Indian lands.

The differences between the French and British systems applied to other things as well. French intellectual leaders such as Voltaire and Rousseau had long used Indian society to measure the faults and virtues of their own, but Jaenen moves beyond them to note that Turgot argued that in the evolution of society itself, the hunting and collecting stage was normal and that Algonkin society was a model of human society at the first stage. In the nineteenth century that concept led Lewis H. Morgan to propound his theory of universal social evolution. Jaenen also finds that the French never pressed Indians to change and that even their Indian reserves were located away from towns and seigneuries with the idea that acculturation could be more gradual. In arguing his case, Jaenen never fails to acknowledge that Indian society was dynamic and vigorous; it interacted with rather than passively accepted European society and culture.

In her very original essay, "The Riddle of Mapmaker Juan Pedro Walker," Elizabeth A. H. John, author of *Storms Brewed in Other Men's Worlds*, demonstrates that a study of the careers of mapmakers can be as rewarding as the study of their maps. Born the son of an English father and a French mother and reared in the Natchez District when it was still under Spanish rule, Juan Pedro Walker learned English, French, and Spanish, showed great talent as a draftsman, and moved in a circle of government and army officials at a time of change and intrigue. The result was that Walker was one of those unknown but able borderland figures whose life constantly intersected with important persons and significant events. As a youth Walker was one of the bright young men Andrew Ellicott hired to assist him in surveying the thirty-first parallel, the boundary that the Treaty of San Lorenzo (Pinckney's Treaty) of 1795 had established between the United States and Spain from the Mississippi to the Atlantic. Later Gov. Casa Calvo asked Walker to survey the Texas-Louisiana border on behalf of Spain after the Louisiana Purchase.

Choosing not to remain in American Louisiana, Walker served in the Spanish army, taught in a military school, and continued to draw excellent maps of the Southwest and Mexico while living in Chihuahua. His maps showed the best understanding to date of the courses of the Red and Arkansas rivers, and it was his luck to serve as the interpreter when Zebulon Pike was interviewed by Spanish commandant general Salcedo after the former was seized by the Spanish when Pike and his men wandered too close to the Spanish province of New Mexico. By then Walker was already a splendid mapmaker, and in the month that Walker and Pike saw one another, John concludes, Pike learned much from Walker's maps, as did his companion Dr. John Robinson. Later the two Americans published maps, of which Pike's was the first to give a "reasonably accurate representation of the rivers of Texas, information that must have come from Juan Pedro."

Besides rescuing Walker and his maps from obscurity and recognizing his influence on the more famous mapmakers of the United States, John throws new light on the way maps played a role in the borderlands struggle for sovereignty over disputed territory. By careful research and wise conjecture she creates for us a Spanish-American borderland in transition that was not a no-man's-land full of desperados but a place where able and informed government and army officers, mapmakers, and diplomats maneuvered to defend their turf.

William H. Goetzmann, professor of American studies and history at the University of Texas at Austin and nationally known author of *Exploration and Empire*, has in recent years been interested in the discoveries made by European and American explorers all over the world. He has called their activities in the eighteenth and nineteenth centuries the "Second Great Age of Discovery," a time when the collection of scientific information went hand in hand with expansion for imperial purposes. In his essay, "Seeing and Believing: The Explorer and the Visualization of Space," he notes that this was a time when the artist and later the photographer were "important components of any serious exploring expedition all over the globe. . . . This was the age that first really visualized the whole earth and its many exotic peoples."

Goetzmann proceeds to illustrate his point by describing the compelling images that such artists as Seymour, Catlin, Bodmer, Miller, and others who painted the American West contributed to a mosaic that eventually formed a single coherent image of the West. Seymour portrayed the vast emptiness of the West, Catlin described it as a paradise of flocks and herds and innocent people, Bodmer dramatized its Indians, and Miller recorded the life of the mountain man in what he saw as a "deeply romantic place." The romantic tone was then truly set by the vast landscapes of Bierstadt and Moran's deliberate choice to paint "sacred places" like Yosemite, Yellowstone, and the Grand Canyon. Looking at photographers as well as painters, Goetzmann concludes that it was the artist of the American West who helped create "the fundamental myth or story of America."

Taken together, these six essays have an unusual unity. Quinn urges us to look again at the earliest settlements to gain a more correct perspective. Dickason talks of the images of the New World in European legal and religious thought, while Fuson demonstrates how scholars themselves created a false image of the accomplishments of John Cabot. Jaenen points out that the French used the image of Indian society to measure the faults and virtues of their own, and John shows how proto-imagemakers such as Juan Pedro Walker described an obscure inland world for curious Spanish and American officials. Finally, Goetzmann limns the complex process by which European and American artists, with concepts of their own, projected those onto a virgin land in paintings that in turn shaped the whole notion of the new world of North America.

Given their unity, their remarkable complementarity, and their demonstration of excellent new scholarship based on new approaches and methods, it is easy to congratulate both the University of Texas at Arlington for sponsoring the Walter Prescott Webb Memorial Lectures, and the presenters whose lectures provided the fine essays for this volume.

DAVID B. QUINN

Colonies in the Beginning:
Examples from North America

IT IS ONLY appropriate, since these lectures are in memory of Walter Prescott Webb, that I should start with a quotation from *The Great Frontier*. "Many explorers," Webb said, "made mistakes in the American wilderness, but nevertheless came back with or sent back valuable information."[1] My subject is in the first place about European governments that made many early attempts to penetrate North America. They made many mistakes. They sometimes learned enough from these mistakes to sponsor viable settlements in the end, but even if the attempts brought back or sent back useful information, for a long time they obtusely failed to learn enough to do so. I can illustrate this part of my topic only empirically from the experiences of England, France, and Spain, though not in that order, and will end my discussion of government policy and the more or less state-sponsored colonizing efforts just at the point in the seventeenth century, in the 1620s, when enduring colonies were finally being inserted into the casually appropriated lands of the inhabitants of the continent, when a "frontier," in Webb's terms, was at last being created, even if I am not going to be concerned with frontier theory as such.

It is a truism, but one we must not lose sight of, that the European colonies in the Americas sprang out of the distinct historical experiences and traditions of each of these states, but it is one that, for my purposes, must be briefly developed. It is, for example, traditional to say that the Spanish empire was born out of the experiences of the *reconquista*, the long process of conquest, town-building, ecclesiastical fervor, and institutionalism that removed Muslim rule from Spain in the very year Columbus sailed, leaving Spain open to venture into the West. While this is basically true, its strict relevance for Spanish activity in North America between 1512 and 1620 is not so clear. By the time North America came within the range of the *conquistadores* the ideals and methods of the *reconquista* had been profoundly modified by earlier enterprises in the New World, first in the Caribbean and then, much more drastically, in Mexico and still more in the conquest of Péru. Consequently, Spanish policy in North America was, in my view, influenced more by these experiences after Columbus's time and by the governmental devices and institutions that evolved to cope with unprecedented problems of government from a distance rather than by anything that had gone before.

Similarly, though in a very different perspective, the activities of both France and England in North America must be seen against the background at home, though here the influences tended to be negative rather than positive. Both nations were held back by more urgent domestic commitments and by lack of institutions which could cope with colonies lying several thousand miles away, and also by lack of capital, which Spain did not lack from the 1520s onward. France, for example, had expelled the English only in the middle of the fifteenth century and had regained a measure of unity only by the beginning of the sixteenth century. In that century France looked to the east and southeast for opportunities for expansion, not to the west, though her seaboard towns did involve themselves deeply in the Newfoundland fishery and were the eventual sources for much of French activity in the western Atlantic. In the case of England the Tudors found themselves fully occupied in reestablishing royal control over their more distant lands in England and in assimilating Wales and attempting, unsuccessfully, to do the same for Scotland, while they were faced with continuing problems in creating some degree of stability in Ireland, which continued until Queen Elizabeth I died in 1603. In the succeeding reign of James I, there were more positive pressures on the part of both merchants and gentry to assert an expansionist policy. Both countries were hampered by religious problems. Henry VIII took over much of the property of the medieval church and Elizabeth had to find means of reconciling most of her subjects to a form of Protestant worship. In France religious wars broke out repeatedly and prevented effective unity in the latter part of the century, until the victory of Henry IV and the Edict of Nantes in 1598 gave France an opportunity to look westward with more effect than hitherto.

I cannot do more here than indicate some of the ways in which these influences, above all governmental influences, affected European attempts to open up North America by exploration for settlement. I may, perhaps, stress too much the mechanisms that governments tried to use to bring about colonial expansion and say too little on the nature of the brief colonial communities that were created and then failed to take root in so many instances. There is often a good deal of documentation on what governments hoped to achieve and too little on what was actually done. Yet as Webb suggested in the quotation with which I began, something in the way of information, and sometimes a great deal, emerged from even the most unsuccessful ventures. Then too, there is a process of learning to be observed, not by any means a continuous improvement in the methods adopted or in the use of the knowledge acquired by earlier attempts, but it is possible to see that something survived from even the worst failures and in the end had enough influence to lead to a measure of success, although even here the amount and nature of the capital investment in colonization had a good deal to do with the narrowing of the margin between success and failure.

There is, obviously, one vital difference, already noticed in general terms, between the position of Spain and that of the other two states. At the time when Spain seriously became interested in North America she already had bases and an organization behind her ventures, first to the Caribbean, where the *audiencia* of Santo Domingo was a continuing if declining source of strength, but more especially in New Spain from the mid-1520s. In Mexico the viceroys had immense resources at their disposal and a substantial degree of autonomy, while at all times the central supervisory machinery created in Spain, the *Consejo de Indias* and the *Casa de la Contratación*, held the initiative and the ultimate responsibility for expansion and determined the form in which successive *entradas* into North America should be made.[2] The major problem is why with such resources Spain did not achieve more and do so more quickly than she did. Her success in so many areas was so spectacular that North America clearly presented unique problems. Basically, they perhaps centered around the slowly appreciated fact that North America did not appear to contain resources that could be exploited both quickly and profitably in areas accessible to Mexico or the Caribbean, however much these areas were to prove such a rich resource to Europeans in later times. More specifically, there were great problems in keeping in touch with expeditions that had apparently disappeared into the unknown, together with the obstructions of a bureaucratic system that often hampered rather than helped operations in which action was the key to success. We must take into account the fact that although interesting information, often embodied in spirited narratives such as that of Cabeza de Vaca,[3] came out of North America, much of the information sent back to Mexico or to Europe was about distances and physical resources and the nature and habits of the indigenous population, and was highly colored and unreliable.

Compared with Spain, both France and England were handi-capped to some extent by the absence of institutions that were con-cerned with overseas developments. The way that Irish affairs, for ex-ample, were handled by both Crown and Privy Council must appear amateurish in the extreme when contrasted with the professionalism of the *Consejo de Indias,* however paper-ridden it tended to become. Much depended on the individual monarch. It is now clear that Henry VII was much more continuously interested in the western voyages than was once believed;[4] Henry VIII had only intermittent curiosity about the new lands when he saw what Spain was getting from her discoveries but did not apply himself to compete. It was not until Queen Elizabeth I had been on the throne for some years that gradually a focus of interest outside and inside her court was created and what we may call an "American" party emerged. It was small but occasionally influential and then only in the last third of her long reign and when she was becoming ever more closely involved in antagonism toward Spain. Thus, English concern with North America in the sixteenth cen-tury may be described as peripheral, and such efforts as were made to intervene there were empirical and lacked effective official support. A very different approach and a more varied, if not immediately more successful, response came with the accession of James I in 1603 and culminated during the next generation.

In France much of the initiative in some significant if intermit-tent achievements came from individual port towns and their mer-chants rather than from the state. This phenomenon was to influence the later forms that French intervention took in America. True, Fran-cis I was personally interested in what lay across the western ocean, but his preoccupation with his European wars and with North Amer-ica as a possible stepping stone to the Pacific governed most of the initiatives he took. The decade 1533–43, indeed, saw some significant initiatives that gave France some presumptive rights over the Saint Lawrence Valley. After 1547 the initiative passed from the Crown to the Huguenot Admiral of France, Gaspard de Coligny, whose at-tempted colonizing expeditions to Brazil in the 1550s and to modern South Carolina and Florida in the early 1560s were of considerable value in bringing information, despite their having only the tolerance if not the full support of the reigning monarchs. There were for many years only a few tentative efforts to maintain French claims, but under Henry IV it was different. As he slowly fought his way to unchallenged power between 1589 and 1598, Henry IV, backed by pressure from towns like Rouen, St. Malo, and La Rochelle, developed a strong sense that a French presence in North America was necessary. But before his murder in 1610 only a little had been done, although what was done was important enough to make France a factor in North American affairs. His successors were to build only slowly on what Henry had begun.

It is well to remember that Spain continued into the seventeenth century to claim prior rights over the whole of North America, though she was prepared to admit some Portuguese rights to Newfoundland and its surrounding mainland areas. The long procession of enterprises that she sponsored in North America gave substance, it might appear, to that claim even if she had so few successes to record. Even if alarm at the increasing ramifications of her commitment led in the 1540s to limitations on new enterprises, her Florida and New Mexico ventures showed that she was not complacent or wholly inactive. Her Florida venture in the 1560s, in particular, gave her a permanent stake in southeastern North America, even if it was a much smaller one than had been intended. Spain continued to base her claim to the widest authority on the papal division of the non-European world in 1493, but as late as 1607, Philip III's minister, the duke of Lerma, could assert that the Americas were "to them *Regum Novum* . . . The division and possession was theirs and therefore lawful both by reasons of nature and nation to appropriate it to themselves and exclude others."[5]

Spain's expectations in North America were not only of gold and silver and jewels; she also expected to create great estates such as had been built up in Mexico, Péru, and elsewhere, based partly on a pastoral economy brought from Spain but primarily dependent on an experienced and servile population of native farmers who would supply, as the people of Mexico and Péru did, the labor force needed to operate estates and mines and also to provide a surplus of food for the urban complexes that were at the core of Spanish society in both the Old and the New World. North America did not do this. Except to some degree in the Pueblo country, Indians were not tied to the soil, even if in many places they grew crops; they were not content to serve as laborers and they resented rather than tolerated alien European intervention and harassed its representatives in most places whenever they could.

The one incentive that remained alive in the Spanish attempt to advance into North America was the missionary impulse. The expansion of Spain in the Indies was considered to be a function of her mission to convert the heathen. This had peculiar connotations in Spanish thinking; it was an important part of Spain's imperial mission and had little relation to the Counter-Reformation. Just as the Jesuits under their Spanish founder had been "soldiers of Christ" in many parts of the Portuguese and Spanish empire, so in North America the Franciscans took their place (the Jesuits indeed retreated in 1572 from all attempts to convert North American Indians). It was the Franciscans who dragged the Spanish forward, hiding their fierce aggressiveness under a cloak of meekness. It was they who eventually made Florida an extended mission field when secular Spaniards had failed to colonize it or to maintain more than a military outpost there, and it was they, as we will see, who involved Spain irrevocably in New Mexico. Part of the ardor of missionary Spain arose from the blood of the martyrs. The Spanish had an impressive roll of them before the end of the sixteenth century — a Dominican on the Gulf Coast, Jesuits on the Chesapeake, Franciscans in the Sea Islands, and another string of Franciscans in New Mexico from 1542 onward. This characteristic masochistic reaction of Christianity to the challenge of heathendom continued to provide incentives to expansion, though it was dulled for a time after the first third of the seventeenth century.

The incentives of both French and English were more prosaic. Both hoped to get through, or in the case of the English, to get around, North America to the Pacific. This was an element in much of the exploration and attempted colonization by both countries. Both set increasing store on the Newfoundland fishery. Although the English were the first to aspire, unavailingly, to take it over in the 1580s, it remained significant in the minds of Frenchmen as well. But from this point the English and French diverged. The English set their minds on the sale to the Indians of English cloth and metal objects but were unsure of what they expected in return. The English convinced themselves that North America in latitudes comparable with those of Spain and Portugal would produce Mediterranean-type agricultural products. They also hoped for metals, precious or otherwise, and so did the French. But the French concentrated on commodities, and to their merchants the fur trade gradually became all-important. Colonization, when it came, had to be fitted into fur trading, while Frenchmen, after countless wars at home, did not for a long time wish to leave France for North America. English men and women proved more willing to leave home; they set their eyes on land, land where they would cultivate exotic crops and richly endow their country and themselves with their produce. Only later in New England did the settlers reconcile themselves to growing English crops and Indian cultivars. English people wished to move as families to new land in North America, in harmony with Indians if they would surrender land to the newcomers, in hostility if they did not. Spain was only interested in the domination of great areas with large estates (if there were no mines), whereas Englishmen were content to exploit small or moderate-sized holdings (larger, however, than they might ever acquire at home). For the French, North America was an area of commercial opportunity, where an adventurous man could make a good living and return with his surplus to France. These are a few of the broad contrasts in the approaches of the three European peoples with whom we are concerned.

What is clear is that Europeans of whatever nation, at most times and places, believed that they had a right to enter and occupy lands in any part of North America they fancied, without any regard for the rights and the safety, even the survival, of those whose possession had been ensured for millennia without interference from the outside. Spanish arrogance in this regard was without comparison. Buoyed by her sense of mission, Spain considered it her duty and her right to occupy non-Christian lands and subordinate non-Christian peoples, even if she did slowly evolve rules that gave them, at least on paper, some legal protection. The English, for the most part, if with some exceptions, followed the same path more slowly, perhaps with less arrogance and less of a sense of mission. The French were the least concerned with disrupting and taking over native territory until missionary activities were added to the fur trade, when she too became involved in the long genocidal process that was to mark European intervention in North America as it had done already in so many parts of the Spanish dominions.

There is a certain degree of irony, even of humor, in the fact that both Spain and England endorsed the first major explorers who were to make an impression in the lands of the western Atlantic with such grandiose paper powers and authority. Columbus, it will be remembered, in the Capitulations and *titulo* of April, 1492,[6] was to be admiral and viceroy of all lands found by him, and to enjoy these offices and pass them on to his heirs, while he was also to have a tenth of all the bullion and jewels he might find. These terms were ludicrously inappropriate to such a minuscule expedition as this when its objective was the Asiatic mainland, where it was known that great empires existed and would present an impenetrable barrier to such a handful of men as Columbus commanded. These articles were to cause endless trouble when his discoveries proved to be only those of primitive and unremunerative Caribbean islands. As for John Cabot, his sons, and successors, the patent granted to them in March, 1496, by Henry VII, accorded them the rights to occupy as governors under the Crown all lands "in whatever part of the world which before this time were unknown to all Christians."[7] These provisions were as unrealistic as those granted to Columbus, even if never realized in any manner whatsoever.

By the time Ponce de León began planning conquests to the north of the Caribbean Spain had begun to plan expansion by grants on paper which both licensed and limited the activities of her *conquistadores* in their *entradas* into new territories. To follow these Capitulations in detail is to see how Spain's concern with North America developed, even if the results hoped for were not achieved and the grantees in practice had little intention of abiding by their contracts, although a few might in the end be punished for glaring failures to do so.

The first Spanish grant to Ponce de León on February 23, 1512, was simple and nontechnical; bureaucracy had not yet come into its own.[8] If he could discover Bimini he could occupy it and make settlements, though fortresses, if needed, would be provided by the Crown. After his first voyage, the Capitulations of September, 1514, were much more formal. By that time, following complaints about the treatment of native peoples in the Islands, a cynical device had been invented to provide a nominal shield for future *conquistadores*. This was the *requerimiento*, a proclamation to be read in Spanish to any concentrations of native people the invaders encountered, which in Spanish (which they could not understand) commanded them to become subjects of Spain and accept Christianity.[9] If they did not acquiesce (and how could they?), then they could be treated as enemies and enslaved or distributed in *repartimiento* (almost the same thing) among the Spaniards. Ponce de León was to use this contract as the first step toward seizing and dividing the land that he had found. Other than some limits to the numbers of Indians that could be assigned to a single Spaniard, the grantee was to have unlimited powers. This grant became, with variations, the pattern for most later Capitulations. But those signed with Ayllon on June 12, 1523, were much more bland.[10] The *licenciado* was to explore lands discovered between thirty-five and thirty-seven degrees north latitude (between thirty-three and thirty-five degrees would be more accurate I believe). There was no mention of the *requerimiento*, although the Christian religion was to be spread by the priests Ayllon was to take with him. Indians were to be taken into service only for wages and were to be treated well; this followed the disgraceful exploitation of captives as slaves in Hispaniola when taken by Ayllon's men in an earlier raid. There was much detail on what sort of colony was to be created. The governor was to have a great estate for himself, but the settlers were to be placed in towns under their own magistrates. He was to pay for this, although subsidies might be given later if he began well. Ayllon did indeed establish the town of San Miguel de Gualdape somewhere on the South Carolina coast, conceivably on the Waccamaw River, but we know more about the quarrels that took place when Ayllon died than we do about the settlement itself. Indeed, it came voluntarily to an end, though many colonists were lost on their way back to the Caribbean. Ponce de León had failed utterly and died of wounds in 1521. Ayllon was only a shade more effective in 1526, even if for a short time a Spanish colony subsisted on North American land.

There was no respite after these failures. Narváez on December 11, 1526, was commissioned to conquer and settle the Gulf coast at his own cost, except for three forts which the Crown would maintain.[11] According to the Capitulations he was not only to be governor-for-life but *adelantado*, a hereditary governor-conquerer (the title had not been granted to his precursors), passing his powers on to his heirs, but accompanied by treasury officials (*oficiales reales*) to see that he paid dues to the Crown. Settlers were to be given grants according to social status, and *caballeros* were to get double quantities of land. His own estate was to be a large one. What was new was the incorporation of a letter dated November 14, 1526, one sent throughout the empire, enjoining governors to protect the rights of the natives and to limit their exploitation of them, although the establishment of missions was to have a high priority.[12] This was a consequence of the growing fear in Spain that labor would be wiped out in the course of conquest, while souls would not be saved from heathendom if cruelty and murder were to be permitted without limitations. Narváez, as is only too well known, failed utterly; his expedition was lost and only the apparently miraculous appearance of Cabeza de Vaca in western Mexico in 1536 brought news of the disaster as well as amazing tales of the interior. This is a case where Webb's dictum, cited at the beginning, holds true.

There was then a breathing space until one of the conquerors of Péru came forward with stolen gold to finance a great *entrada* into North America. The Capitulations made with Hernando de Soto on April 28, 1537, were the most elaborate to date.[13] He was to take on the conquest of all the lands previously granted to Ayllon and Narváez, was to be governor and *adelantado,* and was to establish colonies wherever he could, with assignments to settlers according to rank, outside his own great estate. But he was not to escape some royal supervision: his chief justice was to be appointed by the Crown, as were the treasury officials, while the letter of 1526 was to govern his relations with the native peoples, and he was bound to do his utmost to bring them to Christianity. His great expedition did not get under way until 1539, but its wanderings over much of the southern part of what is now the United States have led historians a dance, as he chopped and changed his plans, moved from one winter quarter to another chasing moonshine gold, making no settlements, and finally dying in the wilderness, leaving Moscoso, daringly, to bring a substantial remnant of his men home in 1543. The contract system had brought no rewards, only disaster.

Two Spanish initiatives differed fundamentally from those covered by Capitulations. The first was Coronado's in 1540.[14] Directed to the supposed Seven Cities of Cíbola, it was primarily an official advance into hitherto unconquered territory. Coronado carried it through effectively (if not without bloodshed), putting the Pueblo country, parts of the Great Plains, and the lower stretch of the Colorado River on the map, but returning with a disciplined force when remaining seemed pointless, without promise of a civilized society in the interior. He did little to support the friars who accompanied him, although a few remained behind to attain martyrdom, but his expedition was efficient and in its way successful in dispelling myths and providing new geographical insights into America. On his return, he was not accorded the honor he deserved.

The second venture of this sort was even more ambitious. Luna was equipped by the viceroy of New Spain in 1559 with a large expedition that was to land on the Gulf coast of Florida and make its way to the coast of South Carolina to take possession of land around the Punta de Santa Elena, where French privateers had been active.[15] Had he done so, the whole of the Florida peninsula would have been secured for Spain. Spaniards and the Indians of Mexico were to become colonists on the land. He was not only to have treasury officials to keep watch on him but he was to consult a junta of his leading men when it was necessary to change plans. Almost everything went wrong, largely because the geographical information brought back by Soto's men was wholly inadequate. We know almost nothing of the temporary settlement at Nanipacana (though a town plan was included in his instructions). We do know that ignorance, misuse of supplies, and inertia prevented any effective move toward the Atlantic coast. Finally, Villa-fañe took over in 1561 and was ordered to take a colony by sea to settle Santa Elena if he could find it. He could not and had to return. Spain had not yet learned how to colonize in North America. In 1561 orders came from Spain that no more attempts were to be made in Florida.

The French Huguenots changed all that. First they settled a small group on Port Royal Sound — the Spanish Santa Elena — in 1562. Although they deserted it in 1563, a larger force under Laudonnière settled on the Saint John's River in Florida in 1564, the possible precursor of many others, as Spanish reports had it. This time a combined operation was planned. Pedro Menéndez de Avilés, an able and rich naval commander, was to be *adelantado* of Florida with wide powers and was to use his own resources as well as the extensive official help to be given.[16] His Capitulations echoed those of his predecessors in other respects. His destruction of the French settlement and the settlers alike left him free to plant soldiers and clergy round the peninsula, establish a base at San Agustín (which had to be moved later), occupy San Mateo, where the French had been, and finally select Santa Elena as a site for a garrison and a city, the latter to be inhabited by tough Asturian farmers. But Menéndez was distracted by other calls for his services; supplies failed several times; the outposts were withdrawn under Indian pressure; and his own great slave-run estate was never laid out. San Agustín lost inhabitants rather than grew (it was laid out, we think, rather on the lines of the plan with which Luna had been entrusted in 1559); the settlers at Santa Elena were harassed by Indians and by the soldiers of the garrison alike. Gradually Florida declined until it was only a chain of small garrisons, despite a further injection of settlers in Santa Elena. After Menéndez's death in 1574, Florida was soon threatened with total desertion as most of the garrison and then all of the Santa Elena settlers departed.[17] But Pedro Menéndez Marqués, the old man's nephew, restored a limited Spanish presence; San Agustín began to grow again. Yet in 1586 Drake cut down San Agustín to the ground and it had to be rebuilt from scratch, while Santa Elena was abandoned. Slowly, San Agustín settled down as a frontier garrison town, kept alive only by new threats of English intervention, and populated mainly by the soldiers' wives, a few merchants and craftsmen, and by Indian-occupied suburbs that provided a market. The town scarcely changed for several generations. But Florida, for all its problems, did become the one solid achievement of Spanish colonization in the sixteenth and early seventeenth century. San Agustín, its plaza, its church and monastery, its tiled houses, and its large wooden fort constituted a genuine accomplishment even if a small one.

Apart from the Luna and Menéndez expeditions, undertaken primarily for strategic reasons, the failure of both Soto and Coronado to found effective colonies or to discover workable mineral resources marked the end of Spanish initiatives in North America for a long time. The New Laws of the Indies in 1542 brought a stronger humanitarian impulse into official policy toward the Indians, even if it did not put a *terminus ad quem* to the holding of Indians in *encomienda*, that is, in tutelage to great landholders. The laws were followed by the setting of a limit to further expansion. In the future there was only to be infilling in areas already under Spanish control, with one elastic proviso: if missionaries penetrated beyond the known limits, then soldiers might be sent in to protect them and their converts. The mission field was not to prove too profitable in North America in the following years. Fray Cancer was killed in western Florida in 1549 when he attempted an unprotected mission; a Jesuit group was wiped out on Chesapeake Bay in 1571 while attempting a comparable venture. Even under protection, Jesuits so completely failed to make converts in Florida that they left the area in 1572. Though the Franciscans penetrated tentatively into Florida in the years following 1573, they made little progress, and their missions were marred in 1576 and 1597 by revolts in which missionary lives were lost. But the urge to persist, to find ways in which they could become effective, survived. In the meantime, the *Recopilación* of the New Laws of the Indies in 1573 offered some fresh cautions and some fresh loopholes for expansion. One notable paragraph stated: "The term 'conquest' is not to be used to describe exploring expeditions. These expeditions are to be made in the spirit of peace and love, and we do not wish them to be described by a word that might be thought to authorize the use of force against the Indians."[18] However, there were provisions for new settlements inside or outside existing borders. The key passages are: "In planning settlements, whether in territory already explored, pacified, and brought to obedience to Us, or in areas to be explored and pacified in future . . . the land should be inhabited by natives who can be evangelized, that being the chief object of settlements authorised by Us."[19] It is then set down that "once the general area has been selected by competent explorers, the sites for principal towns and satellite villages should be chosen. To avoid injury to the natives, they should be unoccupied or freely offered by their inhabitants." At the same time "Indians may be recruited for the new settlements as laborers and craftsmen, provided that they go voluntarily." This was all very humane, if scarcely practical. Indeed, the decree went on to provide that *adelantados* might still be appointed with the rights to hand on their governorship to an heir; they might, if they acquitted themselves well when subjected to the *residencia*, the periodic review of their performance, be entrusted with perpetual ownership of the land and ennobled. Moreover, the *adelantado* might still place Indians in *encomienda* (under legal restrictions on what tribute might be exacted from them) for three generations. The old system was in fact given a humanitarian gloss, genuine on the part of the bureaucrats who drew up the decree, but impossible to enforce at a distance from centers of effective authority. Under these provisions, however, the Franciscan Order, increasingly powerful in Mexico, could continue to exert pressure to expand outward, and to demand civilian protection, even if this meant extending the range of existing authorities in Florida or forcing the civilian authorities to take on new colonizing responsibilities in New Mexico.

Compared with the Spanish initiatives between 1512 and 1543, those of the French look puny. Spain was impelled by the success of her earlier conquests, by the expectation of land and Indians to exploit, of treasure to be found, and not least by missionary aspirations. France, in contrast, had mainly commercial objectives, inspired by Breton and Norman towns and by the desire to find a western way to Asia. Verrazzano did indeed bring the coastline of much of eastern North America to French attention in 1524, but he had found no passage to the South Sea nor indeed did he raise any commercial expectations.[20] But in the late 1520s reports from fishermen suggested that there were water passages into the interior north of Newfoundland. These inspired Francis I to inquire from Pope Clement VII in 1533 if France was excluded from the Americas. The reply, not couched in formal terms, was that as North America had not been found in 1493 France was not excluded from it.[21] When Cartier sailed in 1534 it was to explore these tentative openings, and his exploration of the Gulf of Saint Lawrence might not have had further results had he not brought home Indians from far upstream who inspired further ventures. Cartier did penetrate a thousand miles from the Atlantic in 1535 and survived a Canadian winter at Québec, but he brought only faint hope of passages to the Pacific, though rather more hope of founding a fur trade. Cartier's commission in 1535 merely empowered him to search beyond the New Lands (*oultre les Terres Neufves*), not to appropriate lands or settle.[22] But since Spain was still sending her great expeditions into the interior, even if their failure was not yet known, Francis decided to imi-

tate her at least to the extent of commissioning Roberval as lieutenant general of the lands that Cartier had discovered and authorizing
him to settle them and govern them.[23] Cartier went ahead in 1541 to
prepare the way for settlers, and although he did build a base on the
Saint Lawrence, his men insisted on returning after a single winter.
Roberval, bringing gentlemen and their wives, craftsmen, and con-
victs to labor for him, also managed only a single winter, returning
in disgrace from his strongly fortified settlement, *Francy Roy*, in 1543.
With his return and disgrace, France's attempt to imitate Spain's efforts in North America ended for more than a generation. If the Huguenot colonies, only semiofficial ones, had succeeded, the tale might have
been different.

As for England, there was virtually no enthusiasm for a long time,
although it began to be talked about in the 1550s and a reinforcement
of the Huguenot colony in South Carolina was planned but not carried out in 1563. It was not until the 1570s that a small group of en-
thusiasts for North American colonization appeared. The first English
plans and the revival of French ambitions to appropriate parts of North
America appeared almost at the same time. In March, 1577, Henry
III commissioned the Marquis de la Roche to appropriate such lands
there as he could master,[24] and this was followed in January, 1578, by
a formal commission to him as viceroy of New France, a territory which
was not defined. His attempts to set expeditions on foot in the next
six years came to nothing. But on the English side, the coincidence
in time is striking.

In 1577 a patent to a commercial syndicate to exploit the supposed
gold mines on Baffin Island, revealed in an unsuccessful attempt to
discover a Northwest Passage a year before, led to a spacious grant to
Sir Humphrey Gilbert in June, 1578.[25] This empowered the English-
man to occupy and colonize, with himself as governor with wide powers, lands hitherto unknown to or occupied by any Christians. This
area was too vague for Spanish agents to penetrate for some time, but
it involved in fact a preemptive strike at the North American shores
between thirty-four and forty-five degrees north, a bid to forestall
Spanish Florida from further expansion. Although authorized by Queen
Elizabeth I, the venture was to be a privately financed one. Gilbert
had to find financial assistance where he could. Between 1578 and 1583
he did his best to do so, selling much unexplored land to subscribers
to his ventures, the first expedition never reaching America and the
second in 1583 leading to the formal annexation of Newfoundland,
though no more, followed by his death at sea on his way home. The

transfer of his patent to his half-brother Walter Ralegh in February, 1584, showed that the "American" party at court and among the gentry, with a little support from London merchants, was a serious one.[26]

After an initial reconnaissance, the establishment at the "New Fort" on Roanoke Island of a little more than one hundred men, who survived there in 1585–86 with small loss for ten months, was a significant beginning. This was essentially a colony of soldiers and specialists. The site did not prove suitable for a privateering base against Spain at a time when its mounting hostility to her was leading England into open war. The colony did not discover, any more than comparable Spanish ventures, any important mineral resources. It did find that Indians resented English occupation of their lands, but intensive geographical and other surveys led to discovery of a deepwater harbor, Chesapeake Bay, and land to the south of it not fully occupied by native settlements. Although lack of supplies led the colonists to return prematurely with Sir Francis Drake, the way was paved for a genuine colony of settlement, which was planted in 1587 after many mishaps in the lands that constitute the most southerly part of modern Virginia. These colonists were only occasionally remembered during the long sea war with Spain. They had not been found again before fresh English ventures began in earnest in 1607, having been wiped out shortly before by the jealous Indian overlord of the Virginia Tidewater, Powhatan.[27] The Roanoke voyages did much to create a tradition of attempted colonization, but the objectives of the English differed from those of France and Spain. Hopes of trade with the Indians were indeed raised, but the main emphasis was on settling people, in the belief that England was overpopulated. The colonists were to cultivate Mediterranean and subtropical products, which, it was believed, could flourish between thirty-five and thirty-seven degrees north latitude in North America — olives, vines, sugar, pineapples, and the like — though the Lost Colonists of 1587 hoped that Indian cultivars — corn, beans, and squashes — could provide basic sustenance for the English people who grew them. English hopes of reviving settlement lingered on through the war period and were kept alive by the publication of narratives of the voyagers and colonists.

France was held back from major colonizing activity in America by the wars of religion, especially by the war of succession, 1589–98, but Henry IV, once firmly on the throne, rapidly revived them. He recommissioned La Roche as lieutenant general of Canada, Newfoundland, Labrador, and Norumbega — the whole stretch between about forty and sixty degrees north latitude.[28] This was in direct defiance of Spain and also in competition with English claims. It made sense, for French commercial interests had been expanding. France's share of the fisheries off Newfoundland and the Maritimes had been growing, and her merchants were fur trading in the Maritimes, the Gulf of Saint Lawrence, and the Saint Lawrence River (the summer fur-trading mart at Tadoussac had been active for some years so that to empower some individual with royal authority over these activities was not unreasonable). La Roche, however, concentrated his activities on the commercial exploitation of Sable Island from 1598 onward, but the venture ended in disaster in 1603. Meantime, merchants were given a license to occupy a post at Tadoussac, but it failed in 1600–1601 to establish itself. La Roche was set aside in 1603, since his oversight on behalf of the Crown had had no effect. Pierre du Gua, Sieur de Monts, commissioned for ten years to exploit the territory south of Cape Breton, was to be financed by levies on the Saint Lawrence fur traders.[29] His first colonial site on Sainte Croix Island, near the Bay of Fundy, was laid out in 1604 on civilian lines, but severe weather forced him to move across the bay to found Port Royal. There de Monts developed the characteristic type of French trading settlement, the *habitation* — living quarters and storehouses within a single defensible structure. From there explorers worked their way around the Maritimes and to southern New England. But his patent was withdrawn in 1607 when it became clear that furs in sufficient quantity were not to be obtained in this area. Champlain, employed by de Monts, had shown himself to be a shrewd and effective observer of the geography and resources of the area. In 1608 it was he who was entrusted by the merchants, under royal authority, to found the first permanent settlement on the Saint Lawrence. Québec was established in 1608 with its own *habitation*, copied and developed from that at Port Royal, as the base from which fur trading up and down the river and the lands nearby could be carried on. France was set in her own peculiar mission in North America, which we may characterize as to use as few men as possible to maximize profits. From 1612 there was a nonresident royal governor, but with Champlain as his lieutenant. Before 1627 this was all, except for a few tentative missionary attempts, which came to little. Trudel has called the period down to 1627 "Le Comptoir"— the period when the exchange of goods for furs constituted almost the whole of France's activity.[30] There were plans to do more, but nothing happened until after 1633, when colonization and missionary work began in earnest. France in the sixteenth and early seventeenth centuries showed little consistent desire to stake out territorial claims and to reinforce them by colonies. So long as trade could be safeguarded and developed, that was enough. This differed greatly from the designs of Spain and even of England in this period.

It was Spain that, after its long respite from new adventures in North America, took up again the colonization of New Mexico as her last early venture into the continent. As northern Mexico began to lose its attractions, though its mineral wealth was far from worked out, parties of adventurers made their way from Santa Bárbara northward to the Pueblo region on the upper Rio Grande. These expeditions aimed to explore for minerals and to carry a few friars in search of new Indian communities to convert, even to colonize, between 1580 and 1591.[31] The authorities in Mexico were at first skeptical, then hostile, and finally, largely under Franciscan pressure (the Order being now a powerful force there), inclined toward official intervention. It took some time to find an entrepreneur who would invest his own money in an enterprise that also had official backing and financial support. Oñate finally emerged as such a figure. It took some additional time for him to reach an agreement with the viceroy, Velasco, the contract to which he agreed in September, 1595, being very different in form from earlier Capitulations but reminiscent of them in the new circumstances of the definitions under which new discoveries could be made.[32] The primary document consists of a number of requests from Oñate with answers by Velasco. Most of the requests the latter was able to say that he could accept, provided they were kept within the limits of the printed Ordinances of 1573. These Oñate referred to by number, and it is clear that the viceroy was being very careful to keep within the limitations set down there, which, as it has been shown, were indeed wide enough. But Oñate wanted more than he could be given. Some of his requests were absurdly ambitious; he wished his ultimate authority to extend from the Pacific to the Atlantic and to have his province detached from New Spain and come directly under the *Consejo de Indias* so as to have its own *audiencia* or court of appeal. About these demands Velasco temporized as he had no power to grant them. In any event, he was just winding up his affairs before handing over to the new viceroy, Monterrey, who vigorously repudiated such pretensions and made it clear in his final contract that Oñate was going as a governor subject to recall. In 1598 Oñate finally reached New Mexico and formally annexed it to Spain. His train of soldiers, civilians, and friars (eight of them) had a very mixed experience in the Pueblo country, sending out some useful and some useless reconnaissance missions and installing the friars in many of the pueblos (they took the one they named

Santo Domingo for their own headquarters), while Oñate quartered himself first in one and then in another pueblo. These were not entirely unsuited to Spaniards (reinforced in 1599). Coronado had likened them to the Granada of his day, but we have little information on how daily life was conducted, except that soldiers and civilians for the most part, and some of the friars also, found it intolerable: While Oñate was absent on an expedition in 1601, the greater part of them deserted the colony and retreated to Mexico. Velasco, who returned to Mexico as viceroy soon after, refused Oñate's demands for reinforcements and for punishment of the deserters and eventually relieved him of his office in 1607 but required him to remain at the pueblo of San Gabriel until a final decision could be reached.[33] The Franciscans in Mexico and in Spain pleaded that they had converted so many thousands of Pueblo Indians already (a vast exaggeration if not a downright lie) that Philip III was persuaded to reestablish the colony. Peralta was sent north in 1609 to do so. It was made clear that he was to be simply a salaried governor, subject to orders from Mexico, and his contingent of fifty soldiers, a handful of civilian colonists, and a dozen friars showed that little opposition was expected. The greatly divided Pueblo groups were not inclined to resist. Peralta's main task, as set out in the ordinances, was to establish a city as a nucleus of Spanish power, and so the *Villa* of San Francisco de la Santa Fé was duly established in 1610. We know very little of its character. An adobe church, which soon fell down, official quarters for the governor, officials, and soldiers, and a monastery at least took form around the central plaza. But forced labor had to be used. In the meantime the friars, distributed among the pueblos, were asserting their moral authority over the individual villages, using Pueblo labor to construct churches and serve them in other ways. The Franciscan commissary, Ordoñez, who had followed Peralta, proved to be a man of paranoic ambitions; he declared himself at one point to have all the authority that any pope ever had and soon was treating Peralta as his servant. A grim struggle ensued, the friars dividing soldiers and citizens into two parties. Peralta had lost much of his authority by the time he was relieved in 1614.[34] Although the struggle of church (embodied in the friars) and state (personified by the governor) continued, a *modus vivendi* was slowly established. By means of a strong public relations campaign the friars won official support in Mexico and eventually an assurance of generous supplies for themselves and less generous ones for the officials and soldiers. The colony survived but remained small, except for the attached Christianized Pueblo peoples. They, in fact, became as Catholic as seemed necessary on the surface, while continuing in secret their native religious observances. New Mexico remained an anomaly, hundreds of miles from the Mexican border, never powerful or populous, but a showpiece for supposed Franciscan missionary triumphs. It was to be the last Spanish intrusion into North America for almost a century, and it did little to demonstrate that Spain was prepared to conquer or rule any substantial part of the continent.

The English contribution to North American colonization of course begins with the Roanoke voyages and all the pro-colonization arguments that accompanied them. But it was not until another dynasty took over in England that continuous attention was paid to transatlantic settlement. James I, if inclined to be timid when threatened by Spain, was by instinct imperially minded. He had reason to be: he was the first unchallenged ruler of Ireland for many centuries; he joined the kingdoms of England and Scotland in his person and tried to join them constitutionally as Great Britain. It was almost inevitable that he would assist attempts to penetrate North America. Moreover, there was now merchant capital available in London, permitting the long process of colonization (longer and more painful than had been expected) to begin. The Virginia Company charter of April, 1606, took up where the Elizabethans had left off, but with a difference.[35] Whereas all sixteenth-century grants of monopoly for exclusive trading rights or settlement projects had been solely private enterprises financed by individuals, as were so many of those of Spain, with royal authority remaining in the background, the Virginia charter attempted to join English and Spanish traditions. The companies that would exploit the long coastline between the old limits (thirty-four to forty-five degrees) were to be merchant companies, that of Plymouth to concern itself with Norumbega (the later New England) and that of London with the Chesapeake. Yet, they were to be governed by rules laid down by a royal council, imitating in a sense the *Consejo de Indias*, but composed of relatively minor officials and nonofficial merchants and gentlemen. Settlement was to be financed by the companies, which had much freedom of action, subject to·directives from the royal council. The Plymouth Company's settlement on the Kennebec did not survive more than one winter;[36] it concentrated too much on providing against a French maritime threat, which did not in fact exist, and too little on exploiting the fur trade with expertise that could have been learned from the French or even the local Indians.

The Chesapeake settlement was different. It was to be located well inland and was to concentrate on exploiting indigenous products and reviving the mythical suitability of Virginia for exotic cultivars, while not forgetting to search for minerals. Decimated by disease in the first few months, the colony of little more than a hundred men could do little. Reinforcements in 1608 provoked Indian hostility, which intensified when new settlements were begun by a larger influx of colonists in 1609. The instructions of the royal council did not help.[37] In any event, the existence of the council tended to irritate Spain further, even though she had protested since 1606, and so the second charter in 1609[38] (1) left the London Company to take on some royal powers of direction and, (2) with a further revision in 1612 and the financial assistance of a public lottery in 1613, set it free to experiment. All it could do for some years was to hold on, tightly governing a small community, almost wholly masculine. Until 1616 the colonists were servants of the company and until that year had not sent many useful cargoes to England, but at that point Trinidad tobacco began to provide a staple saleable crop. With the distribution of land to settlers in 1618 and reforms in internal administration, the colony grew, indeed grew too fast to absorb its new settlers. The tobacco boom soon burst. Indians killed many settlers, the company crashed, and the English monarch had to take over Virginia and learn to govern from a distance from 1625 onward.[39]

Virginia is not the whole story, of course. A company colony had done well in Newfoundland in 1610, though less well after a few years, and in 1620 the Pilgrims had, without any effective authority, established their intentionally self-supporting settlement in New Plymouth. Indeed, it cannot be said that really effective English colonies were operating before 1630, but the emphasis on population movements had been established. To move people from England, to make them produce commodities for export, or else to become self-sufficient — these were the established premises of English colonization and the secrets, most probably, of its later success.

In comparing the experiences of Spain, France, and England in North America we are not effectively comparing like with like. The sixteenth century was Spain's imperial century. If she did not develop new capital resources and industry in Spain itself, she obtained them vicariously in the form of precious metals from the success of her imperial ventures in Mexico and Péru. She did not stand at the beginning of a revolution in industry, although it can argued that she, with Portugal, accomplished a revolution in commerce. Yet even here, failures to make an effective impact on North America are puzzling. Had she applied the administrative talents that held her empire together to the systematic exploitation of that area, she could have done much more than she did. Either her bureaucracy was too hidebound to do more than point out guidelines for *conquistadores* that were more of a hindrance than a help, or her agents were not of the stuff that made Cortés and Pizarro the most lucky and successful villains and heroes of early modern history. Essentially, the lack of an amenable labor force in North America was probably the clinching factor in her failures. Without such a force it seems doubtful whether the conquerors of Mexico and Péru could have been more than temporary raiders. They were not the founders of great imperial provinces which had a substantial Spanish and black population to stiffen and support the initial invaders, who in turn were bolstered by the strong network of bureaucratic controls that were placed on them. This sequence did not take place in North America. The networks of missions in both Florida and New Mexico were flimsy substitutes for the tight administrative controls and infrastructure of so much of the rest of the empire. But, however we look at it, the expenditures of so many lives for so little gain and for so much damage to an indigenous society, shows that Habsburg Spain proved ineffective in this particular environment, whether on the east coast or in the interior. We must leave it at that with something of a query in the end; it may be that chance had a good deal to do with it or that there are other factors which have not been taken into account.

Comparing Spain, France (though her population was greater), and England (though her maritime resources were or became substantial), the capacity of any of them effectively to penetrate and control any substantial parts of North America was almost insignificant. Yet, the accumulation of capital in the French port towns and cities (in Spain matched only by a small area in the north of the country) enabled them to reach out to the natural resources of the more northerly parts of North America and to glean wealth from both fish and furs, and, for long, to do so without disrupting, even though influencing, aboriginal society. In the end missionaries were to alter this and eventually the state was to take a hand, but that was beyond the period with which we are dealing. The French state, as such, did not assert itself as an imperial power during this early period.

England was, again, somewhat different. She was concerned with financing privileged corporations from the midcentury onward, but they were not directed to the western Atlantic but to Muscovy, the Levant, and eventually to India and the Far East. The East India Company brought home its first rich cargo three years before the first charter was granted to the Virginia Company. The eyes of a substantial number of Englishmen were indeed directed toward the west in the last quarter of the sixteenth century, but their actual efforts were puny and ineffective, except in so far as they provided precedents for more effective action early in the following century. The state was too short of money and resources to aid merchants' private western ventures. Yet, after the war was over in 1604 it became possible to mobilize merchant and gentry capital to make a major drive into the Chesapeake. If it emerged in the end that the privileged commercial corporation was not the correct instrument for doing this, the lesson had to be learned and was learned by experience, often bitter experience. But behind the slow and significant growing mercantile power of England, the desire of a sufficient number of her people for new land and for new opportunities did give her expansion an advantage over the efforts of France and even of Spain to insert her presence significantly into eastern North America. There were factors, not touched on here, that contributed to her success there, notably religious ones, which came into operation effectively only from 1630 onward. But by that time her teething troubles were already almost over, and she had become the first effective North American colonizing power.

I think that the comparison tells something about government. Spain, having virtually invented (in modern times at least) government from a distance, was obsessed with paper. Her officials really did think that rules set out on paper could and would control the men and their followers engaged in penetration of untraversed areas in North America, and that when they were ready to settle there, that they could be influenced by being told what to do. The somewhat dreary episodes we have pursued do, I think, show that this did not work. The French, on the other hand, were skeptical about the effects of bureaucratic intervention. For a moment in 1541–42 they may have felt that Roberval could establish a living colony in Canada. After that, even if they set up viceroys and their lieutenants to do things in America, they never cared much whether they did anything or not. They were not concerned with the workings of bureaucracy; they were affected by what pressures important merchant groups could bring on them, and this is how French Canada got started in its own peculiar way. How it changed in the 1630s is not part of my story here.

As for the English, their rulers were prepared to go through the motions of handing out charters but not to supervise their operation, but to let nature, in the shape of men like Gilbert or Ralegh, take its course. If they failed, so much the worse for them. In the one attempt between 1606 and 1609 that was made to insert a bureaucratic element into the colonizing process, it took only from April, 1606, to May, 1609, to demonstrate that this was more a hindrance than a help. The merchants and their supporters had to go ahead without government intervention. That too was to begin changing in 1625 and thereafter. But for the period with which we are concerned, I think the comparison will stand.

This topic, I am sure, should form the opening chapter in any attempt to survey the European penetration of North America. Its tentative character contrasts sharply with the following period of rapid development and change, so that it may be tempting to begin a course on the Colonial Period in 1607 or 1620, but this, I strongly believe, is misleading. The scale of European enterprise in North America before these dates is such that it must form the correct introduction to what follows; the subsequent history of North America cannot be fully understood unless this is done. I hope I am preaching to the already converted, but if not, I hope that they will take what I have said to heart and that students and lecturers alike will understand how vital the pre- and protosettlement periods are to the understanding of what came after.

NOTES

1. Walter Prescott Webb, *The Great Frontier* (Austin: University of Texas Press, 1963; London: Secker and Warburg, 1963).

2. The basic textbook on the administration of the Spanish empire remains Clarence H. Haring, *The Empire in America* (New York: Oxford University Press, 1947).

3. Alvar Núñez Cabeza de Vaca, the English version of whose "Relation" is in David B. Quinn, Alison M. Quinn, and Susan Hillier, *New American World. A Documentary History of North America to 1612*, 5 vols. (New York: Arno Press and Hector Bye, 1979), II, 15–59, translated from *La relactión qui dio Núñez Cabeza de Vaca* (Zamora: Augustín de Paz and Juan Picardo for Pedro Musetti, 1542). Additional report in Quinn, *New American World*, II, 59–89.

4. See ibid., I, 91–123.

5. David B. Quinn, "James I and the Beginnings of Empire in America," *Journal of Imperial and Commonwealth History* 2 (1974): 146.

6. In English, Samuel Eliot Morison, *Journals and Other Documents on the Life and Voyages of Christopher Columbus* (New York: Heritage Press, 1963), pp. 27–30.

7. In Latin and English, H. P. Biggar, *The Precursors of Jacques Cartier* (Ottawa: Public Archives of Canada, 1911), pp. 7–10.

8. Capitulations with Pedro Ponce de León, in English, Quinn, *New American World*, I, 231–33; in Spanish, *Colección de documentos inéditos de Indias*, 1st series (42 vols. Madrid, 1864–84), XIII, 26–32. There is a brief overall view of these arrangements for North America in Eugene Lyon, "Spain's Sixteenth Century North Ameri-

can Settlement Attempts," *Florida Historical Quarterly* 59 (1980–81): 275–91, the main focus being Florida.

9. In English, John H. Parry and Robert G. Keith, *New Iberian World. A Documentary History of the Discovery and Settlement of Latin America to the Early 17th Century*, 5 vols. (New York: Times Books and Hector and Rose, 1984), I, 285–90.

10. Capitulations with Lucas Vásques de Ayllon, in English, Quinn, *New American World*, I, 249–53; in Spanish, Fernández de Navarrete, *Obras*, 4 vols. (Madrid: Biblioteca de Autores Españoles, 1964), II, 102–107.

11. Capitulations with Panfilo de Narváez, in English, Quinn, *New American World*, II, 4–10; in Spanish, *Colección de documentos inéditos de Indias*, 1st series, XXII, 224–45.

12. In English, Quinn, *New American World*, II, 6–10; in Spanish, Archivo de Indias, Seville, Justicia 750A, ff. 236–87.

13. In English, Quinn, *New American World*, II, 93–96; in Spanish, Buckingham Smith, *Colección de Varios Documentos para la Historia de la Florida y Tierras Adyacentes* (London: Trübner, 1857), I, 140–46.

14. Fully documented in George P. Hammond and Agapito Rey, *Narratives of the Coronado Expedition, 1500–1542* (Albuquerque: University of New Mexico Press, 1940). The appointment of Francisco Vásques de Coronado is extracted in English, pp. 83–86; in Spanish, in *Hispanic American Historical Review* 20 (1940): 83–87.

15. The expedition of Tristán de Luna is fully covered in Herbert I. Priestly, *The Luna Papers, 1559–1561*, 2 vols. (Deland: Florida State Historical Society, 1928), instructions in Spanish and English, I, 18–43; in English also in Quinn, *New American World*, II, 207–11.

16. Capitulations with Pedro Menéndez de Avilés, in English, Quinn, *New American World*, II, pp. 384–89; in Spanish, *Colección de documentos inéditos de Indias*, 1st series, XXIII, 242–58. See especially Eugene Lyon, *The Enterprise of Florida, 1565–1568* (Gainesville: University Presses of Florida, 1976); he prints a supplementary contract of March 15, 1565 (Lyon, *Enterprise of Florida*, pp. 213–19).

17. Documents in Quinn, *New American World*, II, 277–471; see also David B. Quinn, *North America from Earliest Discovery to First Settlements* (New York: Harper and Row, 1977), pp. 240–61.

18. Parry and Keith, *New Iberian World*, I, 368.

19. Ibid., I, 370–71.

20. Lawrence C. Wroth, *Voyages of Giovanni da Verrazzano* (New Haven, Conn.: Yale University Press, 1970), is the authoritative narrative.

21. Charles-André Julien, *Les voyages de découverte et les premiers Etablissements* (Paris: Presses universitaires de France, 1948), pp. 115–16.

22. H. P. Biggar, *Collection of Documents Relating to Jacques Cartier and the Sieur de Roberval* (Ottawa: Public Archives of Canada, 1930), pp. 44–45 (in French).

23. Ibid., pp. 178–85.

24. Alfred Ramé, *Documents inédits sur le Canada* (Paris: Librairie Tross, 1867), 2nd series, pp. 6–10 (in French).

25. David B. Quinn, *The Voyages and Colonising Enterprises of Sir Humphrey Gilbert* (London: The Hakluyt Society, 2nd series, nos. 83–84, 1940), I, 188–97.

26. David B. Quinn, *The Roanoke Voyages, 1584–1590* (Cambridge: The Hakluyt Society, 2nd series, nos. 104–105), I, 82–89.

27. David B. Quinn, *Set Fair for Roanoke* (Chapel Hill: University of North Carolina Press, 1985), pp. 341–78.

28. Marc Lescarbot, *History of New France*, ed. W. L. Grant and H. P. Biggar, 3 vols. (Toronto: Champlain Society, 1907–14), II, 196–201.

29. Ibid., II, 211–26. The narrative by Samuel de Champlain forms the basic source. Champlain, *Works*, 7 vols. (Toronto: Champlain Society, 1922–36), I, 233–469. See David B. Quinn, "The Preliminaries to New France. Site Selection for the Fur Trade by the French," *Wirtschaftskräfte und Wirtschaftsweg* (Nuremburg: In Kommission bei Klett-Cotta, 1978), IV, 9–25.

30. Marcel Trudel, *Histoire de la Nouvelle France*, II. *Le Comptoir, 1604–27.* (Ottawa: Fides, 1906); Champlain, *Works*, II, 1–226, contains the crucial account of the establishment of the French on the Saint Lawrence, 1608–12.

31. These are fully documented in George P. Hammond and Agapito Rey, *The Rediscovery of New Mexico, 1580–1594* (Albuquerque: University of New Mexico Press, 1966).

32. The agreements between Juan de Oñate and the viceroy, Luis de Velasco, are in George P. Hammond and Agapito Rey, *Oñate: Colonizer of New Mexico*, 2 vols. (Albuquerque: University of New Mexico Press, 1952), I, 42–64. The volumes contain all that is known about New Mexico between 1584 and 1609.

33. Ibid., I, 32–35. A Spanish study of Oñate's venture, Luis Navarro García, *La conquista de Nuevo Mexico* (Madrid: Cultura Hispanica del Centro Ibero-américano de Cooperación, 1978) heads its last chapter "Tierra de Desencanto."

34. Pedro de Peralta's instructions of March 30, 1609, were printed by Lancing B. Bloom, "Ynstrucción a Peralta por Vi-Rey," *New Mexico Historical Review* 4 (1929): 178–87, although the translation is not too reliable. The best-documented study of Peralta's experiences at the hands of Fray Isidro Ordoñez is France V. Scholes, *Church and State in New Mexico, 1610–1650* (Albuquerque: Historical Society of New Mexico, Publications in History, No. 7, 1937), pp. 19–67.

35. April 10, 1606. Quinn, *New American World*, IV, 197–98.

36. David B. Quinn and Alison M. Quinn, *The English New England Voyages, 1602–1608* (London: The Hakluyt Society, 2nd series, no. 161, 1983), pp. 376–468.

37. December 10, 1606. Quinn, *New American World*, V, 197–98 (May, 1609), mistakenly placed under the second not the first charter; Quinn, *New American World*, V, 212–18. The fullest documentation is in Philip L. Barbour, *The Jamestown Voyages, 1606–1609*, 2 vols. (Cambridge: The Hakluyt Society, 2nd series, nos. 136–37, 1969).

38. Second charter, May 23, 1609; third charter, March 12, 1612. Quinn, *New American World*, V, 204–12, 226–32.

39. The history of the Virginia Company is pungently described in Edmund S. Morgan, *American Freedom: American Slavery* (New York: Norton, 1975), pp. 44–130.

ROBERT H. FUSON

The John Cabot Mystique

JOHN CABOT was, and is, an enigma. For more than three hundred years he was generally regarded to have been an elderly merchant who remained in Bristol while his son, Sebastian, engaged in epic voyages of exploration. The "Sebastian supremacy," as James Williamson calls it, culminated in 1831 with the publication of Richard Biddle's *Memoir of Sebastian Cabot*.[1] Within a few years documents were revealed that indicated that a terrible historical mistake had been made. John had made the discoveries for England, not Sebastian! By the late nineteenth century the pendulum had swung the other way: John had become the hero and Sebastian, a charlatan and weaver of fables. The "John Cabot mystique" had begun to take shape.

One hundred four years have elapsed since Henry Harrisse set out to correct the historical record and to restore John to his proper place among fifteenth-century navigators.[2] Dozens of books and articles have appeared during the past century as scholars sorted through the old records and pored over the early nautical charts. The last significant find came as recently as 1956, when Dr. L. A. Vigneras discovered the John Day letter in the Archivo General de Simancas.[3] Nevertheless, in spite of all of this attention to the Cabots, our ignorance is appalling.

We do not know where John Cabot was born, when he was born, or even his exact name. There were no contemporary portraits or physical descriptions that we know of, so his appearance is a mystery. No extant document informs us of his residency before he went to Venice. Only fragments of his family life have come down through the years; his father's name is in doubt, and nothing is known about his mother, two of his sons, or his brother.

No one can say when he departed Venice, and no document reveals anything about his maritime experience (if any) before or during the Venice residency. We are uninformed about what transpired after John Cabot's leaving Venice and before going to England. The year of John's arrival in England is not certain, nor are we positive about which city there was his first home. His arrival in Bristol is also un-documented.

John made a short, unsuccessful voyage in 1496, but all details of it remain a secret. There is no absolute date for the departure or return of the 1497 voyage, and the North American landing site has never been determined.

Lastly, we do not know when John died, where he died, or how he died. His death may have been at sea or anywhere on land between Canada and Florida.

Such is the stuff that makes good historical fiction, if not good history. John Cabot, unfortunately for us, was born into a world that did not keep very good records for persons of humble origin. Biographies of such men came later, after the accidents of history and geography thrust fame and fortune upon them. But John's untimely death permitted little of either. John Cabot himself left not a single holograph scrap — not a letter, not a map, not a ship's log. Nothing. Nothing, that is, except Sebastian.

The few bits and pieces of biographical information that we have are derived from certain Venetian civic records, casual references in letters mailed by contemporaries from England to correspondents in Italy and Spain, some household accounts from England, and statements made by Sebastian. Usually the latter were to people who did not know the senior Cabot personally, and Sebastian clearly kept alive memories of his father's real or imagined exploits by assigning the credits to himself.

So thoroughly did Sebastian absorb John's identity that Richard Eden, one of England's greatest sixteenth-century writers, who knew Sebastian well, was unaware that John had ever commanded a voyage for Henry VII.[4] Further, Peter Martyr, Spain's counterpart of Eden, was also personally acquainted with Sebastian and wrote of the alleged epic voyages to discover the Northwest Passage. But Martyr never mentioned John's 1497 journey to Canada and, seemingly, had never heard of it.[5] This is comparable to Las Casas' forgetting that there ever was a Christopher Columbus and assigning the discovery of San Salvador to Fernando!

It appears that no one in England had heard of John Cabot before 1495, no one saw him again after 1498, and almost everyone had forgotten him by 1513, the year that Polydore Vergil completed his *Anglica Historia*.[6] Here is a man that many regard as the first post-Viking visitor to Canada and that some consider to be the true discoverer of Florida, yet the incontrovertible facts allow him only three years of

English service, during which time he failed in two-thirds of the voyages he attempted.

If we sift the verifiable materials pertaining to John Cabot, we derive only a small residue of absolute truths: (1) John became a Venetian citizen between 1471 and 1473, after having resided in Venice for at least fifteen years; (2) he had at least one brother, Piero, and a Venetian wife, Mattea; (3) his father was named either Egidius or Giulio, and had been a merchant; (4) by 1484 John had at least two sons, one of whom was Sebastian; (5) between 1490 and 1493 a Venetian named John Cabot Montecalunya was in Valencia and Barcelona and may have been the historical John Cabot; (6) John was in England no later than 1495; (7) John Cabot was in London before going to Bristol; (8) on March 5, 1496, Henry VII granted letters patent to Cabot and his three sons, Lewis (Ludovico), Sebastian, and Soncio (and to their heirs and deputies) to discover and investigate lands in the eastern (i.e., East Asian), western, and northern sea; (9) John made his first English voyage from Bristol as commander in 1496, but was forced to turn back; (10) he made a second voyage in May, 1497, in the bark *Matthew*, with a crew of eighteen to twenty, including at least two Bristol merchants and two old friends; (11) a landing was made somewhere west of Ireland in June, 1497; (12) Cabot returned to Bristol in August, 1497; (13) a third voyage, with five ships, sailed from Bristol in May, 1498; (14) at least one ship from the 1498 fleet turned back from Ireland; (15) John Cabot never returned from the 1498 voyage.

These are the bare bones of John Cabot's life and his enterprise. Meat may be added to the skeleton, but only at the risk of introducing controversy. One need only turn to the exhaustive studies of the last century to ascertain the depth of the disagreement.[7] Generally, no two Cabotian scholars have been able to come to total agreement on such matters as the number of voyages, dates of the voyages, and landfalls (among other things) because of (1) national, provincial, or personal biases, and/or (2) the role of the cartographic evidence.

BIAS

Of the principal Cabotian scholars, only James A. Williamson and Theodore E. Layng seem to have been able to thrust subjectivity aside and rise above it. Williamson said, "The problem should be kept strictly objective."[8] And, ". . . there are those who allow themselves to form a prejudice, a conviction that there is not evidence to clinch, such as that the shore first discovered, Prima Tierra Vista, 'must have been' in Newfoundland, or in Nova Scotia, and warp their thinking to this end; or a personal animosity such as Henry Harrisse conceived for Sebastian Cabot, who became for him an unmitigated villain and the liar who plunged John Cabot's story into the obscurity that covers it. Such are the snares that beset the Cabot student. He must be alert to keep the critical, even skeptical, mind and see the evidence for what it is truly worth."[9]

Layng, in a similar vein, stated, "In such a subjective study I have found that an idea must be allowed to simmer for some time before presenting it for public consumption."[10] "Cabot scholars," noted Layng, "are an intractable lot, each insistent upon the rules by which the game must be played but none of them ready to submit to an umpire."[11] Quoting G. R. F. Prowse, Layng goes on to say, "if I appear in other respects to have gone 'beyond the pale,' I can only repeat the subject is 'subjective to the nth degree.'"[12]

Prowse, writing to W. F. Ganong, with whom he had corresponded for forty-six years but never met, said, "It is the fate of us poor devils writing pre-history, subjective to the nth degree, to become sologists. However, if we were not chockful of pre-possession, highbrows call them theories, our work would lose much of its interest."[13]

Provincial Bias. Prowse and Ganong, Canadian scholars, fought the battle of Newfoundland versus Nova Scotia.[14] Prowse once said, "For many years my dear friends Biggar and Ganong carried on with me a vigorous correspondence. At times from 1895 to 1940 I exchanged letters almost weekly with Ganong in our endeavour to solve problems like the landfalls of John Cabot, the exploration of the Gulf of Saint Lawrence, and where the original Labrador was. The work of Dawson, Biggar, and Ganong was scholarship of the highest class. Naturally Ganong with his United Empire Loyalist connection and the Prowses' several centuries connection with Newfoundland gave us both an unavoidable bias."[15]

National Bias. In addition to a scholarly tug-of-war between Canadian provinces as to where Cabot first landed, there are also examples of national claims. Inasmuch as the so-called European discovery of North America was a continuum (for five hundred years and maybe longer), there are a host of nationalistic opportunities for anyone wishing to enter a claim for *the* discoverer.

Portugal assigns the discovery of North America to João Vaz Corte-Real, in 1472. All one has to do to learn this is to stroll down the beautiful Avenida da Liberdade in Lisbon and read the inscription in the mosaic sidewalk: "Descoberta da América, 1472" and "João Vaz Corte-Real, Descobridor da América."[16] Naturally, Brazil accepts the Portuguese version, but surprisingly, so does Argentina.

Denmark, Norway, and Sweden also recognize the 1472 date but usually say that Corte-Real was an observer on a ship piloted by Jon Scolp (Johannes Scolvus) and under the joint command of Hans Pothorst and Diderik Pining. The Scandinavians, of course, can always fall back on the Viking voyages.

Armando Cortesão was firmly convinced that his Portuguese countrymen mapped the Antilles in 1424 and indeed discovered them before that date.[17] James E. Kelley, Jr., has recently lent strong support to this idea, and even goes so far as to suggest that some of the mapped "legendary" islands were the North American mainland proper.[18] If he is correct, Nova Scotia and Florida appeared simultaneously on the Nautical Chart of 1424.

In the United States the Columbus discovery is the official one, but at least one Canadian is certain that Columbus was in Newfoundland and Nova Scotia as early as 1477.[19] The Portuguese, I am sure, will hasten to point out that at that time Columbus was sailing for them.

The French, to the best of my knowledge, have never filed a claim for a pre-Columbian discovery of North America. But Henry Sinclair (St. Clair) of the Zeno Narrative was of French descent, and some place him in Newfoundland and Nova Scotia ca. 1395. Further, there is pretty good evidence that Breton fishermen were working the Grand Banks in the fifteenth century.

The Irish had Saint Brendan (all Irish captains were saints!) in the sixth century, and they can certainly muster a good argument that those intrepid curragh-paddlers preceded the Vikings wherever the latter went. And there are some in Florida that swear that the Welsh prince Madoc discovered Tampa Bay ca. 1170 and landed in Saint Petersburg.

Perhaps the Italians have the best national claim. Their men captained the first important exploration ships for the Spanish, French, *and* English, and Marco Polo beat everyone to Cathay.

National rivalry, however, had its deadly serious aspect, producing, for instance, the Treaty of Tordesillas, an interesting geopolitical instrument that gave Portugal title to Brazil before that land was even discovered. It was not binding on nonsignatory states, contrary to popular opinion, nor did it obstruct England's voyages to the west.[20] The confusion over the location of Newfoundland, mapped by the Portuguese (Cantino, 1502, for example) as east of the Line of Demarcation, may have resulted from poor surveys rather than political intrigue. It may also have caused increased activity among the Portuguese to place João Vaz Corte-Real there as early as 1472 in order to establish validity to the post-Cabotian discoveries made by his sons. Interestingly, the Juan de la Cosa chart of ca. 1500 does not indicate the Line, nor do any Spanish maps for the next quarter century.

National interests also appear to have caused a rewriting of history or even the creation of it on occasion. The English Crown really did not concern itself with what the pre-Cabotian Men of Bristol did, or even pay more than scant attention to the sanctioned voyages of John Cabot at the time. Later, when Jacques Cartier reached Canada in 1534, England had cause to review its Canadian claims. There was a pattern of juggling the historic facts to move English territorial claims ever farther southward. In other words, if John Cabot did actually discover (or rediscover) Labrador in 1497, then it would have behooved the English to rewrite history and place the landing in Newfoundland or Nova Scotia.

The serious national claims to eastern Canada by the Portuguese, English, and French clearly affected the scholarly output for many years. Ethnocentrism may still be found in the literature, and the Anglo-French competition in modern Canada is not unrelated to the question of who discovered North America and/or who established a valid claim.

Personal Bias. This last type of bias was displayed by Henry Harrisse in his treatment of Sebastian Cabot, of whom he wrote, "it is certain that we must consider him as a dishonest man, capable of disguising the truth, whenever it was his interest to do so."[21] Prowse went even further in the third volume of his *Cartological Material*, with an essay titled "Sebastian Cabot Lied."[22] In volume IV he stated that "this miserable scoundrel [Sebastian] robbed his father of this northwest passage idea. . . ."[23] Harrisse and Prowse openly despised Sebastian to the point that it affected their objectivity.

Layng held no love for Sebastian either. He once said that "Sebastian Cabot should be expunged from the text books. . . ." Nevertheless, Layng also stated, "I acknowledge a common denominator of genuineness running through various reports emanating from S. Cabot of an early English voyage to northern regions."[24] But Layng hoped that this voyage would prove to be one of John's, thereby eliminating the contentions of Sebastian. There is, of course, nothing wrong with a scholar calling a spade a spade, but even rascals sometimes tell the truth, and one's prejudice cannot be allowed to suppress these occurrences.

David O. True represents a different category of personal bias.[25] His Cabotian studies appear to have been motivated by his anti-Spanish feelings. Though he stated many times in his correspondence that "English ideals and methods and peoples are superior to the Latins," he really meant "superior to Spaniards and Spanish-Americans."[26] He clearly excluded the Portuguese from his detestation, for João Fernandes was a virtual saint, and some Italians, such as John Cabot, were acceptable. But Cabot had had enough vision to immigrate to England, and True was immovable in his belief that Sebastian was born there. True further saw no harm in Sebastian's going to Spain in 1512, where he served two terms as pilot-major before returning to England in 1548. Could it have been that Spain's pilot-major was an English-born citizen who was, in reality, an agent for the English Crown? True obviously thought so.

Christopher Columbus, on the other hand, was despicable, for he threw his lot in with Spain and the Catholic church, and True saw a conspiracy with the two "spreading a net that engulfed even our friend [Samuel Eliot] Morison."[27] In a letter to Williamson, True wrote, "If I am right in my belief that Cabot discovered Labrador before Columbus found the West Indies, it seems of increasing importance that we use this fact to emphasize our Anglo-Saxon heritage. I am dedicated to the belief that we are doing much more than to recite the history of where John Cabot went. We are bringing cohesion to our English-Canadian-American relations, realizing that we are all an undeclared commonwealth of English speaking people. To arrive at a reasonable solution of what John Cabot really did has been not only a challenge *but a mission* [italics mine], for which I have practically discarded every other interest."[28]

True set out to prove that in the fifteenth century the English rediscovered North America, a birthright derived from their Nordic (i.e., Viking) forebears. True places John Cabot in Labrador 105 days before Columbus reached San Salvador. In a series of voyages, True has Cabot discovering everything along the Atlantic and Gulf coasts, from

Canada to Mexico. David True did not embark on a project to learn who discovered what; his enterprise was to prove a foregone conclusion — the English were first.

True built a Procrustean frame for his hypothesis and forced the few subjective pieces of Cabotian material to fit it. His voluminous correspondence to every Cabotian scholar active between 1946 and 1964 provides a clear indication that he was not interested in listening to or reading others' ideas. True's letters were to win converts for what had become a crusade and to instruct them. To Williamson he wrote, "I am satisfied that there is no evidence of value that does not fit my present outline," and, "1497 was Cabot's first (successful) voyage only for the uninformed."[29] Referring to the scholar who discovered the John Day Letter, True said, "Vigneras has a good mind, as I know, but he has not been in touch with Cabot materials for any length of time, nor with other Cabot scholars."[30]

The cartographic record was treated in the same cavalier manner by True. Virtually every anonymous map constructed in the early sixteenth century was assigned to John Cabot, Sebastian Cabot, or to João Fernandes (whom True believed to be John Cabot's pilot). The so-called "Columbus Map," described by Roncière in 1924, was credited to John; Kunstmann II was given to Sebastian; Cantino was attributed to Fernandes, and so on.

Those maps that showed Asia or merged Asia with the new western discoveries, such as Cantino (1502) and a whole line of Lusitano-Germanic successors were, to True, maps of eastern America. Every Portuguese name from Labrador southward was seen to emanate from Fernandes. In this manner True was able to land John Cabot at Hamilton Inlet on June 29, 1492, and place him in downtown Miami fifteen years before the voyage of Juan Ponce de León.

The tremendous flow of correspondence to Williamson, immediately prior to the publication of the latter's 1962 book on the Cabot voyages, causes me to believe beyond a shadow of a doubt that Williamson was directing these words to True, when he wrote,

> Some yield to the fascination of maps, wildly incorrect maps as they obviously are, and strive to extract from them secrets which for the most part they do not contain. The Cabotian map-scholar has too often allowed his mind to become permeated with the idea that the early sixteenth-century maps were designed primarily to give information about John Cabot, whereas in fact the cartographers may have known little or nothing about his voyage and many not even have heard his name. This is a form of self-deception unrecognized by its victim and increasing its

influence as his mind becomes more absorbed in the study. His minutely detailed scholarship becomes ever more admirable, while his judgement of the broad implications of evidence decays. Those who have read much in the Cabot literature of the past century will not be at a loss for examples.[31]

True's research, done at home and in almost total isolation, and faulty to the point of disbelief, has nevertheless had great impact on Cabotian studies in Canada and has even worked its way into history texts in Florida. It was still making front-page news in Miami as recently as March, 1983.[32]

True's "mission" to restore Anglo-Saxon hegemony to North America by discrediting Hispanics in general and Columbus in particular would accomplish the following, if anyone took it seriously: (1) The pre-Cabotian Men of Bristol would be denied their rightful claim to the rediscovery of Canada; (2) Juan Ponce de León would be struck from the historical records of Florida and reduced, along with Columbus, to second-class status; (3) Florida would acquire a new "first" map of itself, the Cantino of 1502; and (4) Florida would inherit an incorrect map for its first post–Juan Ponce representation (the Freducci) and a wrong date for that map (1514).

MAPS

Overdependence on cartographic evidence and misinterpretation of it are symptomatic of an affliction that has been almost epidemic among Cabotian scholars. If there is very little documentary material, there is a rather abundant cartographic record. Extant are at least fifty maps made before 1520 that show some part of eastern Canada.[33] For those of us who have spent years researching the first voyage of Columbus, this represents a complete reversal in the kinds of source materials. With Columbus we have used a hefty pile of written evidence to create a single map of his discoveries; Cabotians have used numerous maps to reconstruct the written record.

Most Cabotian scholars have turned first to the famous (or infamous, depending upon your point of view) map of Juan de la Cosa (1500 ?). Upon its foundation have been erected all sorts of theoretical structures. Layng stated it well when he wrote, "It is generally accepted that the first line to be laid down in the cartography of Canada was an east-west line in approximately the same latitude as Bristol. This line, presumably relating to the exploration of John Cabot in 1497, is represented on the La Cosa chart (1500) from what is known as the 'named' coast. A similar line is also present on the Oliveriana map (1505–1509). This now famous named coast of the La Cosa map has become a reef upon which scholars have delighted to run aground."[34]

Layng used the word "presumably" when referring to the named coast of Cosa and its association with John Cabot, for there is no proof that there is a connection. Prowse thought that the nomenclature came from Hugh Eliot and Robert Thorne, who may have been the first known Englishmen to visit Canada. There is also no guarantee that the map was drafted in 1500 (clearly, the eastern half was not), nor that Juan de la Cosa was the cartographer. There is even doubt as to whether there were one or two Basque mariners named Juan de la Cosa.

Regardless of the problems endemic to the Cosa chart, it is the only Spanish world map extant before the Turin map of 1523. No *original* Portuguese map is known prior to that of Pedro Reinel (1503), and there is no post-Columbian Catalán map of the New World. The English do not seem to have worried about charts before the 1520s, and the Irish left only legends. Other than a chart of the African coast (probably made in 1490) there is no original chart from western Europe for the period 1487–1500.[35]

The so-called "Columbus Map" described by Roncière *may* be pre-1500. It is certainly not the work of either Christopher or Bartholomew Columbus, and John Cabot had nothing to do with it. Kelley thinks it is probably of Venetian origin.[36] Newfoundland is on this map, but it appears to have been added at a later date, judging by the lighter linework. Further, it does not look as though it was drafted by the same cartographer who produced the main map. Especially odd and unexplainable is the partial erasure of a legend next to the lightly drafted Newfoundland, a legend that must have been on the original. The legend reads "HEC SEPTEM CIVITATUM INSULA VOCATUR, NUNC PORTUGALENSIUM COLONIA EFECTA, UT GROMITE CITANTUR HISPANORUM, IN QUA REPERIRI INTER ARENAS ARGENTUM PERHIBETUR" (Here is the island called of the Seven Cities, a colony now peopled by Portuguese: it is said from a report by Spanish ship-boys that silver is found there in the sand).[37]

There is no way to ascertain if Newfoundland was on the map before or after Cabot's 1497 voyage, but if the map is pre-Cosa (1500) it could be the first cartographic record of Canada.[38] The Cosa chart has an erasure on its continental coast, next to the named coast, which apparently makes reference to the Seven Cities. Both erasures indicate some confusion among either the cartographers or later users. The legendary Island of the Seven Cities seems to have first been the Azores. It later wandered all over the Atlantic from the West Indies to Newfoundland; and it eventually reached the American Southwest.

John Cabot was not in the New World long enough to make anything like a detailed survey. He undoubtedly named certain features, but if the Cosa chart represents Cabotian nomenclature, it has obviously been muddled by someone. Since Cabot made only one trip to Canada (1497), he had nothing to do with the naming of Labrador. Labrador of the early maps was Greenland; the name did not find its present geographic location (modern Labrador) until many years after Cabot.

I am unwilling to accept the notion that Labrador-Greenland was named for João Fernandes, the so-called *labrador* from the Azores. Assuming that an early explorer were to ignore his religion and/or national sponsor, he would hardly resort to assigning nicknames to significant places. Columbus, for instance, was very careful to establish a precise hierarchy for naming his discoveries: (1) God, (2) the Virgin Mary, (3) the king, (4) the queen, (5) the heir to the throne, (6) the country he represented. Further, Columbus used the language of his employers when giving names. Cabot himself would never have used Portuguese.

Every Cabotian scholar has overlooked the fact that *Labrador* is a Portuguese synonym for *Cérbero*, the mythical three-headed dog that guards the gates of hell.[39] The word is also synonymous with intractable, impractical, unmanageable, and severe, or with a vigilant and brutal guardian. What is more, there is a northern constellation by that name. Laborer or landowner is a rare synonymous usage, restricted to one who manages salt-producing lands. I would suggest that the three islands at Kap Farvel (Cape Farewell), Greenland, might logically be associated with the gates of hell. What better place to have a "vigilant and brutal guardian"! Were Greenland named for João Fernandes it would more likely have been called Terra de Fernandes.

An additional word or two concerning nomenclature is required. Other than the name "Newfoundland," which first appears as "the new Isle" in its evolutionary development toward "new founde Launde" (by 1502), Cabot left virtually no linguistic traces on the Canadian shore.[40] The Cosa names are secondhand; English explorers would not have named a sea (whether it be the Gulf of Maine or that of Saint Lawrence) the "Sea Discovered by the English" (*mar descubierto por inglese*). The mapmaker knew that the English had made the discovery, but he did not know what they had called the feature. The Spanish is much too poor to have been from Juan de la Cosa or any other literate Spaniard and the nomenclature suggests a strong Catalán influence.

This hint is one point in favor of John Cabot Montecalunya and John Cabot Bristol being one and the same. If the Bristol John Cabot was originally Catalán, then we set the stage for place-names that could easily be botched by a Castilian copyist. It also lends great weight to Prowse's theory that *Bonavista* was the first landing site, for Bonavista is a Catalán word in its purest form. The only town in Europe named Bonavista is in Catalonia. [41]

Another pure Catalán word is *Cabot*. It is odd that no scholar has ever remarked on this fact. Cabot is a common Catalán family name, filling columns of the modern Barcelona telephone directory. It is easy to pronounce in English but is always altered in Spanish, Italian, and dialects such as Genoese and Venetian. In keeping with Catalonian (and Spanish) custom, a person named Joan (John) Cabot Montecalunya would be known as Cabot, dropping the last (i.e., mother's) name. For some reason never understood by me, the Catalonian people and their language have been all but ignored by scholars, except those few who are deep into portolan chart history.

I suggest, in sum, that there is a good possibility that John Cabot was a Catalonian, perhaps from Bonavista — what a good name to give to your first Canadian landfall! Cabot later moved to Venice and became a naturalized citizen, but he returned to the land of his birth briefly before moving to England.

But why leave Spain? If Williamson is correct in placing John Cabot Montecalunya in Valencia and Barcelona in 1493 (and if our two Cabots are one and the same), we are able to establish a motive for moving to England. [42] In the spring of 1493 Cabot could have seen and even met Columbus, who was passing through the area with his entourage of Taino Indians. Cabot knew his Marco Polo well enough to realize that the few primitive artifacts and naked brown people he saw were *not* what Polo had described. Columbus had stopped short of Asia! It was still awaiting an Atlantic approach. Inasmuch as Portugal was committed to sailing there by way of South Africa, and Spain was obligated to stay with Columbus, there was only one viable alternative — England.

John Cabot may have gone to England in 1494 or early 1495. He probably went first to London, then to Bristol. Here he learned that the Men of Bristol had already done what Columbus had done — failed to journey far enough. But the Men of Bristol were not looking for

Asia. They may have been seeking the legendary Isle of Brazil or the Island of the Seven Cities, or perhaps nothing more than a good fishing hole.[43] In any event, Cabot was successful in obtaining permission to sail *beyond* Brazil and the offshore islands found by the Spaniards. Once at the mainland a turn south would fetch Cathay. Also, the distance was less in these northern latitudes.

Such a northern voyage to a point beyond any European discovery would not have violated the terms of the Treaty of Tordesillas (which the good Catholic King Henry VII fully respected), it would not have been a rediscovery of something every sailor on the Bristol waterfront already knew, and it would have made Bristol the spice capital of the world.

Cabot's idea was a solid one, based on a true global concept of great circle sailing. He may have gotten beyond "Brazil" in 1497, but not much beyond. His untimely death, either at sea or somewhere in eastern North America, in 1498 brought an end to the dream.

Cabot, like Columbus, never knew that he was on a new continent. Both men were dead before Europeans finally grasped the concept of a major obstruction between them and Cathay, probably around 1510 or so. But some cartographers kept the Asian idea alive until the middle of the sixteenth century.[44]

John Cabot was quickly forgotten and his brilliant plan for a short route to Asia could not compete with the actual successes of the Spanish and Portuguese. The later attempt by the English to resurrect Cabot's discovery no more impeded Cartier and the French than Drake's claim to California would slow the Spaniards in their advance. Failure to follow the 1497 voyage with colonization was the greatest geopolitical mistake the English could have made.

There will always be an aura of mystery surrounding John Cabot. That frequently happens when things are left unfinished and virtually no explanation accompanies them. That he was an exceptional man, there can be no doubt. Why else would so many of us write so much about one of whom we know so little?

NOTES

1. James A. Williamson, *The Cabot Voyages and Bristol Discovery under Henry VII* (Cambridge: The Hakluyt Society, 2nd series, no. 120, 1962), p. 96.

2. Henry Harrisse, *The Discovery of North America* (London and Paris, 1892; reprint, Amsterdam: N. Israel, 1961).

3. L. A. Vigneras, "New Light on the 1497 Cabot Voyage to America," *Hispanic American Historical Review* 36 (1956): 503–509; and "The Cape Breton Landfall: 1494 or 1497," *Canadian Historical Review* 38 (1957): 219–28.

4. Williamson, *Cabot Voyages*, p. 95.

5. Harrisse, *Discovery*, p. 27.

6. Williamson, *Cabot Voyages*, p. 224.

7. For a complete bibliography of pre-1964 Cabotian studies, see W. F. Ganong, *Crucial Maps in the Early Cartography and Place-Nomenclature of the Atlantic Coast of Canada*, with an introduction, commentary, and map notes by Theodore E. Layng (Toronto: University of Toronto Press, in cooperation with the Royal Society of Canada, 1964). For general bibliography and specialized cartographic references, see W. P. Cumming, R. A. Skelton, and D. B. Quinn, *The Discovery of North America* (New York: American Heritage Press, 1972); and Seymour I. Schwartz and Ralph E. Ehrenberg, *The Mapping of America* (New York: Harry N. Abrams, Inc., 1980).

8. Williamson, *Cabot Voyages*, p. 67.

9. Ibid.

10. Theodore E. Layng, letter to David O. True, September 28, 1955.

11. Layng, "Introduction," *Crucial Maps*, p. xiii.

12. Ibid., p. xvii.

13. Ibid., p. xii.

14. Prowse and Ganong were two of the most important Cabotian scholars but were men of almost opposite personality and persuasion. Layng provides a fascinating biography of both in his introduction to *Crucial Maps*, pp. ix–xvii. Complete bibliographies are on pp. 478 (Prowse) and 499–501 (Ganong). Prowse's studies, typed and mimeographed by his own hand (even to the age of eighty-five), offer many autobiographical glimpses of the scholarly recluse. Though the men never met and never used first names, they agreed that, upon their deaths, all of their correspondence over a forty-six-year span and all of their Cabotian papers would be placed together in the New Brunswick Museum at Saint John.

15. G. R. F. Prowse, "Cartological Material. IV. Voyages" (Winnipeg, 1944), p. 3 (mimeographed).

16. Ian Cameron, *Lodestone and Evening Star* (New York: E. P. Dutton and Co., 1966), p. 114.

17. Armando Cortesão, "The North Atlantic Nautical Chart of 1424," *Imago Mundi* 10 (1953): 1–13.

18. James E. Kelley, Jr., "Non-Mediterranean Influences That Shaped the Atlantic in the Early Portolan Charts," *Imago Mundi* 31 (1979): 18–35.

19. Pedro Bilbao, "Was Columbus in Canada?" *Américas* 18 (1966): 17–28.

20. Henry Harrisse, *The Diplomatic History of America* (London: B. F. Stevens, Publisher, 1897), pp. 43–48.

21. Harrisse, *Discovery*, p. 27.

22. Prowse, "Sebastian Cabot Lied," in "Cartological Material. III. Names" (Winnipeg, 1942), pp. 1–28 (mimeographed).

23. Prowse, "Cartological Material. IV. Voyages," p. 15.

24. Layng, letter to D. O. True, September 28, 1955.

25. David O. True (1885–1967) went to Miami in 1933, after losing a fortune in the stock market. Although he had graduated from Colgate (1909) and done graduate work at Chicago (1909–10), he was too busy earning a fortune in the investment bond business to pursue historical studies. The Crash of 1929 gave him the time, but very

little money, to begin his quest. The thirties were devoted mostly to looking for sunken treasure ships, but by 1943 he turned his energies to Florida history and began to assemble his vast collection of photocopied maps. His interpretations of fifteenth- and sixteenth-century charts led him to form a hypothesis that John and Sebastian Cabot made seven voyages for England between 1491–1499, reaching Labrador in 1492 and Florida in 1498. True's publications include:

   1944   "The Freducci Map of 1514–1515," *Tequesta* 4:50–55.
   1944   editor of reprint and revision of *Memoir of Fontaneda*, University of Miami and the Historical Association of Southern Florida.
   1954   "Some Early Maps Relating to Florida," *Imago Mundi* 11:73–84.
   1956   "Cabot Explorations in North America," *Imago Mundi* 13:11–25.
   1960   "New Light on the 1492 Voyage of John Cabot," *The Carrell* 1:13–14.
   1961   "John Cabot's Maps and Voyages," *Actas* 2, Congresso Internaciónal de História dos Descobrimentos, Lisbon.

True's extensive collection is housed in Special Collections, University of South Florida Library, Tampa.
   26. David O. True, letter to Thomas Dunbabin, April 19, 1960.
   27. True, letter to L. J. Jackman, May 1, 1961.
   28. True, letter to J. A. Williamson, March 1, 1962.
   29. True, letter to J. A. Williamson, January 4, 1962.
   30. Ibid.
   31. Williamson, *Cabot Voyages*, p. 67.
   32. Howard Kleinberg, "Miami: The Way We Were," *Miami News*, March 12, 1983, and March 19, 1983. Kleinberg, editor of the *Miami News*, received numerous awards for his outstanding series of articles on early Miami history. True's controversial theories are presented as an episode in recent Florida history, especially the debate he touched off by claiming that Miami was the first place visited by Ponce de León. Kleinberg's approach is totally objective.
   33. Layng, "Introduction," *Crucial Maps*, p. 473. For a chronological listing and commentary on these maps see Theodore E. Layng, ed., *Sixteenth-Century Maps Relating to Canada* (Ottawa: Public Archives of Canada, 1956).
   34. Layng, *Sixteenth-Century Maps*, p. xiii. For one of the best discussions ever put forth concerning the Cosa chart, see Ganong, *Crucial Maps*, pp. 8–43 and 469–72. Also see Williamson, *Cabot Voyages*, pp. 72–83 and 295–307. Additional insights on the Cosa map are in G. R. Crone, *Maps and Their Makers: An Introduction to the History of Cartography* (London: Hutchison's University Library, 1953); and G. E. Nunn, *The La Cosa Map and the Cabot Voyages* (Jenkintown, Pa., 1946).
   35. Heinrich Winter, "On the Real and the Pseudo-Pilestrina Maps and Other Early Portuguese Maps in Munich," *Imago Mundi* 4 (1947): 25–27; Crone, *Maps and Their Makers*, p. 80.
   36. James E. Kelley, Jr., letter to author, March 29, 1983; Charles de le Roncière, *The Map of Christopher Columbus* (Paris: Les Éditions Historiques et Édouard Champion, 1924). True believed this to be a map made by John Cabot. True, "New Light on the 1492 Voyage of John Cabot," *The Carrell*, between pp. 12–13.
   37. Roncière, *Map of Christopher Columbus*, pp. 27–28. See also Cortesão, "North Atlantic Nautical Chart," p. 8; W. H. Babcock, *Legendary Islands of the Atlantic* (New York: American Geographical Society, Research Series No. 8, 1922).
   38. Kelley believes that the map *could* be as early as 1470 (letter to author, March 29, 1983). He agrees with Cortasão that Roncière's argument for a Columbus origin is "fan-

ciful." I am in complete agreement with Kelley that the absence of the West Indies has no real bearing on the date; I am equally convinced that Newfoundland is an addition at some date after the original construction. The reference to the Seven Cities suggests a fifteenth-century date, but the best indicator of a pre-1500 date is the well developed "Saharan snake," a feature characteristic of early Catalán charts. This feature, looking somewhat like a scaly serpent and stretching east-west across North Africa, appears at least as early as ca. 1291–1330, on a chart prepared by Giovanni (Mauro) di Carignano in Genoa. Currently located in the Real Archivo di Stato di Firenze, it is fully discussed in Paolo Revelli, *Cristoforo Colombo e la Scuola Cartografica Genovese*, Consiglio Nazionale delle Ricerche, (Genoa: Stabilimenti Italiani Arte Grafiche, 1937), II, facing p. 208. The "snake" is well developed on the Angelino Dulcert map of 1339 and may derive from Herodotus. See E. H. Bunbury, *A History of Ancient Geography* (New York: Dover Publications, 1959), I, 172–276. Kelley believes that the "snake" is the "common representation of the Atlas Mountains in Catalán cartography." I do not concur, but feel that the so-called "ridge of sand" referred to by Herodotus is the origin and, geographically, it makes sense. This "snake," incidentally, is depicted on the Juan de la Cosa chart, indicating a Catalán origin or influence. Disallowing, for the moment, the Vinland map and the 1424 Nautical Chart, Newfoundland may have been mapped on the Pietro Roselli chart of 1447 (Revelli, *Cristoforo Colombo*, facing p. 280). Certain symbols resembling islands (seven?) appear due west of the Breton Peninsula. These may represent Canada.

39. *Dicionário Geral de Sinônimos e Locuções da Língua Portuguêsa*, 2nd ed. (Rio de Janeiro: Biblioteca Luso-Brasileira Ltda., 1960), I, A–F, 525; II, G–Z, 1396.

40. Ganong, *Crucial Maps*, p. 39.

41. Francesc de B. Moll, ed., *Diccionari Català-Valencià-Balear* (Palma de Mallorca, 1964), II, 573. Village attached to the district of Pla del Penedès.

42. Williamson, *Cabot Voyages*, p. 40. "Montecalunya looks like a place-name, but all efforts to trace it or anything like it in Italy and Spain have so far failed." Montecalunya is both a place-name and a proper name. It was a common practice to identify a person by his place of origin (i.e., Fernández *de Oviedo*). Montecalunya is the name given to the forested hills near Barcelona. According to Francesc de B. Moll (*Diccionari*, III, 48): "P. Aebischer ha documentat extensament les més antigues aparicions del mot *català* i ha suggerit com a possible una nova explicacío de l'origin del mot: Catalunya es derivaria de *Monte Catanu*, forma medieval de *Montcada*, que degué generalitzar-se com a nom del pais per esser aquell la muntanya principal del comtat s'havria derivat un nom de pais *Catalonia;* que s'havria canviat en *Catalonia* per analogia d'Aragonia." (P. Aebischer has documented extensively the oldest appearance of the word *català* and has thereby suggested a possible new explanation of the origin of the word: Catalunya [English = Catalonia] is derived from *Monte Catanu*, a medieval form of Montcada, which became a generalized name of the country because it was the principal mountain of the county [earldom] of Barcelona; from *Catanu* an adjective, *catananu*, was formed; from *catalanu* was derived a name for the country, *Catalonia;* the change in *Catalonia* is analagous to that of Aragonia.) Names denoting origin or mother's family (occurring as a "last" name) are dropped in English-speaking countries.

43. It is estimated that Spain had an average annual income of less than $2 million (1966 dollars) from her exploits in America, yet Portugal realized more than $5 million (1966 dollars) a year from her fisheries on the Grand Banks (Cameron, *Lodestone*, p. 124).

44. Cantino (1502) is the earliest survivor of a series of maps that Harrisse referred to as "Lusitano-Germanic." The series included, among others, Caveri (Canerio), Ruysch, Schoner, Waldseemüller, the Lenox Globe, Contarini-Roselli, and Stobicza. The 1492 globe of Martin Behaim also belongs in the group, and probably the chart of Juan de la Cosa, if not in nomenclature at least its closed "Asian" coast. As late as Vopell (1558) the American mainland was thought to be Asia. Schwartz and Ehrenberg (*Mapping of America*, p. 18) state that the Cosa chart is "the earliest extant map showing any part of the continent of North America." Actually, Cosa placed jumbled names on what he thought was Asia, and the configuration of the named coast may be from an earlier "guesstimate" of the Asian coast, not a survey of the North American one. Further, the claim by Schwartz and Ehrenberg that Cantino is "the first map to present Florida as a peninsula" cannot be substantiated. If the so-called "northwest coast" in Cantino is not Asia, then it is Yucatán, Central America, or even eastern Canada.

OLIVE PATRICIA DICKASON

Old World Law, New World Peoples, and Concepts of Sovereignty

THE SPECTACULAR EXPANSION of Europe's geographical horizons during the fifteenth and sixteenth centuries was crucial to the development of international law. This is evident in the work of Dominican Francisco de Vitoria (1486?–1546), primary professor of sacred theology at the University of Salamanca; Alberico Gentili (1552–1608), regius professor of civil law at the University of Oxford; and Hugo Grotius (Huigh de Groot, 1583–1645), jurist and diplomat, who published his epoch-making *De jure belli ac pacis* in 1625. An examination of the thought of these men reveals that even as they weighed the implications of the discoveries, either directly or indirectly, they still all worked within legal traditions that were already centuries old by Vitoria's time. The purpose of this essay is to examine, however briefly, the development of the concept of sovereignty in Europe and how it was applied in relation to certain of the territories and peoples of the New World during the Age of Discovery. It will be seen that while thinkers disagreed about the extent to which Christians held priority over non-Christians in temporal as well as in spiritual affairs of state, a consensus nevertheless developed, on secular and humanistic grounds, that New World peoples did not possess sovereignty. Although the two colonizing powers that will be considered here, Spain and France, were both concerned about the legitimacy of their positions, and although each was committed in principle to the rule of law and the universal right of access to that law, neither ever seriously doubted its right to assert its dominion over the lands and persons of Amerindians.

The issue of sovereignty had been engaging the attention of European canonists (experts in church law) at least since the twelfth century and civilists (experts in civil law) since the thirteenth, when the discovery of the Americas toward the end of the fifteenth century dramatically enlarged and altered the perspectives of the debate. In political terms, the problem involved the ideal of universalism that had once been expressed by the Roman Empire versus the regionalism of emerging nation-states. In ecclesiastical terms, it concerned the powers of the pope as head of the universal church, vis-à-vis the temporal powers of the emperor and national monarchs. The issues had been complex enough when debated within the context of Latin Christendom (Europe had been predominantly Christian since the days of Charlemagne), but when Western Europeans began to contest control of the Holy Land with the Saracens, questions that had not been satisfactorily resolved, or perhaps not seriously considered, took on a new importance. Did non-Christians possess natural rights to property? Did their rulers exercise legitimate authority? In short, did unbelievers possess *dominium* (lawful possession of property and political power)? Were Christians justified, indeed, did they have a duty to wage continual war against infidels (a term which at that time primarily meant Saracens)?[1]

Expanding geographical knowledge added further dimensions to these issues. First, there was the dawning realization that in Asia and Africa there existed nations scarcely known to Europeans, only a few of whose inhabitants were Christian; then came the discovery that in the western ocean between Europe and Asia there existed lands totally unknown to Europeans, whose inhabitants had not only never *heard* the Christian gospel but had never even heard *of* it. What was the status of these peoples, and what were their rights? Specifically, were Europeans justified in claiming the "rights of discovery" over their lands and in waging wars of conquest against them? Surprising as it may seem in the light of what actually happened in the New World, an important segment of canonical opinion, both before and after Columbus's voyages, upheld the rights of non-Christians to property and to their own governments, and further, that wars could be waged against them only for a just cause.[2] Some canonists went so far as to deny that any war could be considered "just," as war by its very nature injured the innocent as well as the guilty.

The principal scholastic authority for upholding the rights of non-Christians was the canonist Sinibaldo dei Fieschi, who as Innocent IV was pope from 1243 to 1254, and for restricting them, Henry of Segusio, cardinal of Ostia (d. 1271, generally known as Hostiensis). To begin with Innocent IV, he held that all rational creatures, Christian or non-Christian, had the right to own property and to exercise political authority in their own lands: "possessions and jurisdictions can lawfully exist . . . among pagans, for these things have been made not only for the faithful but for every rational creature . . . it is not permitted to the Pope, or to the faithful, to take away either their lordships or jurisdictions from the pagans, which they possess without sin. . . ."[3] However, since the authority of the pope extended to all people, whether or not they acknowledged Christ, he did have the right to intervene on behalf of Christian subjects who were being abused by a non-Christian ruler, particularly in domains (such as the Holy Land) where Christians had once held jurisdiction:

> but also against other pagans, who now hold land, in which Christian princes have had jurisdiction, the Pope may justly make a rule, and decree that they must not unjustly molest Christians who fall under their authority. . . . If they should illtreat Christians, he can sentence them [the heathern rulers] to be deprived of their jurisdiction and lordship. However, it must be a grave cause which would come to that, for the Pope should support them as much as he can, provided there should not be danger to Christians, nor a grave scandal brought about.[4]

If a non-Christian ruler presented a threat to his Christian subjects' religion, then Innocent IV was unequivocal that the pope could depose him from office, on the grounds of misuse of power. If possible, this should be done by persuasion (including monetary inducements) rather than by force, as the legitimacy of the ruler's office was not being challenged.[5]

Although Innocent's argument supporting the legitimacy of power outside the church and even outside of Christianity established its case on theoretical grounds, in the practical arena the laurels went to the opposite view, *extra ecclesiam non est imperium* (there is no legitimate authority outside the church). Apart from the principles that were considered to be involved, non-Christians governing Christians was an emotional issue. Scriptural support against tolerating such a situation was discerned in Saint Paul's stand against Christians appearing before non-Christian judges.[6] It was popularly believed that since the dominion of infidels could never be just it was always permissible to wage war against them.[7] This was the extreme version of the position championed by Hostiensis, a leading member of the Sacred College, and an associate of Innocent IV. Although on many points he was in accord with *"dominus meus,"* as he referred to Innocent, he took issue with him on the recognition of non-Christian right to power over Christians. According to Hostiensis, "infidels, neither recognizing nor obeying the power and authority of the Roman Church, are not fit to have kingdoms, governments, jurisdiction nor dominion."[8] Non-Christian rulers could not possess dominion de jure but only de facto:

... whence we steadily assert that by right infidels should be subject to the faithful, and not the reverse . . . we allow, however, that infidels who recognize the authority of the church are to be tolerated by the church; nor are they to be absolutely forced into the faith. . . . Such people may have possessions and Christian dependents and even jurisdiction by the toleration of the church.[9]

Toleration was possible only if heathen rulers did not abuse their Christian subjects, and then only to the extent necessary to avoid persecution: "But also, if they illtreat Christians, [the pope] can sentence them to be deprived of the jurisdiction and dominion which they have over them."[10] Patience was advised: "where Christians live under the jurisdiction of infidels whom they are not able to resist, then they must possess themselves with patience, and in practice recognize the infidels' jurisdiction."[11] In the tradition of such advocates of papal power as Alanus Anglicanus (fl. thirteenth century), Hostiensis contended that the Church was God's channel for all power, spiritual and temporal. The pope possessed "plenitude of power" which the cardinal described as the "supreme and surpassing superiority and power and authority [which] has been granted to him without reservation in all matters. . . ."[12]

Such views naturally led to questions about the relationship between temporal and spiritual powers. The great Dominican synthesizer, Saint Thomas Aquinas (1225?–74), pondering Aristotle's thought that recently had been reintroduced into Europe via the Arabs, concluded that temporal or natural law (*jus naturale*), which was discernible by human reason, was an aspect of eternal law (*jus aeternum*), which was beyond human comprehension.[13] He agreed with the Greek concept of natural law as a criterion of right conduct residing in nature, beyond the control of man or state. That part of it which was applicable to human conduct, *lex naturalis*, was promulgated in each man through his nature.[14] All mankind shared in natural law, and all types of states came within its orbit. Saint Thomas, concurring with Aristotle that the natural objective of a state was the material well-being of its citizens, sought to correlate this with the Christian ideal of absolute justice, a system higher than that of either natural law or man-made (positive) law. Although he saw temporal power as being separate from spiritual power, and even accepted the autonomy of the state in temporal matters, Thomas did not put either of them on an equal footing with the spiritual authority of the church.[15]

Saint Thomas, in synthesizing Greek with Christian thought, and incorporating elements of Roman jurisprudence, had provided ammunition for each of two principal views of human society: that it was a unified whole receiving its right to governance directly from God, and that it was a collection of diverse entities each receiving its right indirectly from God through the people. The first of these lines of thought supported the theory of papal supremacy which would prevail over the conciliarist movement during the later Middle Ages. The second would find a congenial atmosphere at the University of Paris, where Thomas himself had taught and where his student, John of Paris (ca. 1240/41–1306), also a Dominican, would develop this aspect of his teaching. John held that religious and political worlds were separate entities, each with its own standards. Because man is by nature a political or civil animal, it is natural for him to live in a community in the form of a state or kingdom under the direction of one person concerned with the general good. Community life was based on natural law, of which the law of nations (*jus gentium*) formed a part, quite separate from religion.[16] In John's eyes, the society of man was fundamentally human, but not necessarily Christian.[17]

A next step for this line of thought was to assert the complete secularity of political power. Marsilius of Padua (1270–1342), rector of the University of Paris, did this in his book *Defensor Pacis*, published in 1324. Marsilius held that as God was the author of nature, he was an object of faith and hence outside the realm of political science.[18] He saw the power of the state as arising solely from the people, whether they were Christian or not; sovereignty rested in them, while only spiritual matters rested in the church. Marsilius thus freed natural law (*jus naturale*) from divine sources, and its expression in human society (*lex naturalis*) from the necessity of a Christian purpose. In his words, the state was "living nature," an expression of the will of its citizenry.[19] The ruler, deriving his power from the consent of the people, was sovereign in his own domains.

In ecclesiastical circles also, the concept of universalism was under attack. The Franciscan William of Ockham (1299?–1349) followed a line of reasoning similar to those of John of Paris and Marsilius when he said that since all societies were subject to natural law, religion could not be used as a criterion for their legitimacy. Pagan societies, too, could be founded on right, as the power of a nation-state could be secular. Such thinking encouraged the emergence of politics as a social science rather than as a branch of theology.[20]

As these theoretical debates on the nature of political authority progressed, they provided national monarchs with a rationale for contesting the authority of the universal powers of pope and emperor.

England's Edward I (reign, 1272–1307) and especially France's Philip IV (1285–1314) both asserted sovereign rights against Pope Boniface VIII (1294–1303); eventually, the monarchs prevailed.[21] In 1312, the Holy Roman Emperor, Henry VII (1312–13), found Robert of Naples (1309–43) guilty of *lèse majesté*. Since Robert's kingdom was technically a fief of the papacy, the latter took his case against the emperor to Pope Clement V (1305–14), who found in favor of the king. By that important act Clement officially endorsed for the first time the principle of national sovereignty in temporal matters against that of the Holy Roman Empire.[22] This ruling helped to set the stage for the confrontations that would characterize Europe's colonial expansion.

A precursor of these confrontations occurred on the eve of the Age of Discovery when Poland sent Paulus Vladimiri (Pawel Włodkowic z Brudzewa, ca. 1370–1435), rector of the University of Krakow, to the Council of Constance in 1414 to begin a long battle against the Teutonic Knights, an order founded in 1198 to wage war against infidels in the defense of Christianity. Polish authorities had turned to the university for help in its campaign to prove that the Order had long since lost sight of its original purpose and had become enmeshed in pursuing its own aggrandizement even at the expense of Christian peoples. This had happened when the Order had begun to acquire Polish territories in 1308; it had taken Poland a century before it had been able to stop the process, in 1410. Vladimiri, an established scholar and experienced diplomat, argued that neither the propagation of the faith nor the papal plenitude of power provided sufficient justification for waging war against the infidel and depriving him of his dominion.[23] He held that infidels within their own domains were subject only to natural law and not to Christian positive law, whether canon or civil, and that wars could not be waged justly against them by reason of unwillingness to accept Christianity.[24] Since the Order had waged such wars, it had unjustly deprived infidels of their legal rights, and should be compelled by the Council to make restitution.[25] Vladimiri's position contradicted what had become the accepted medieval practice of expanding Christianity by the sword as well as by the word. In view of the fact that the papacy had tacitly supported the Order for two centuries, Vladimiri diplomatically resorted to the evidence of history to prove that the Order had not only behaved very badly but had also used the faith to disguise its self-interest when doing so. In the end, he rejected warfare altogether as an instrument for the extension of Christianity, as even so-called "just" wars spread misfortune and destruction.[26] He urged the Council to reject as "wicked and against reason" the doctrine denying unbelievers their rights under natural law and sought to have those rights, as taught by Saint Thomas Aquinas, enshrined in positive law binding upon all Christians.[27] Although Vladimiri did not carry the day, his systematization and marshaling of his arguments on juridical, theological, and historical grounds foreshadowed international law, just as the issues he addressed foreshadowed those which were to arise with the discovery of the Americas.

To summarize briefly, until the age of European overseas expansion, the question of the nature of sovereignty was argued primarily in theological terms, as the principal concern was whether or not Christianity was essential for the legitimacy of a ruler. While most clerical thinkers continued to maintain that it was, a substantial body of opinion supported the view that it was not, that a non-Christian prince who behaved in accordance with natural law was fully entitled to rule. But even the secular theory of sovereignty left many loopholes for Christian aggression; according to the practice that developed in the New World, Christians, provided they were acting on behalf of their monarchs, could take Amerindian territories and force the inhabitants to accept baptism.[28]

The ambiguities in European political theory can be observed in the Spanish Crown's move to obtain Rome's sanction for its claims to Amerindian territories in return for Spain's promise to evangelize. This followed a procedure that had been established well before Europe became aware of the existence of the Americas.[29] Spain had previously received the Canaries as a papal grant (1344), and in 1455 Nicholas V (pope, 1447–55) had awarded Portugal control of non-Christian lands on the West Coast of Africa, to name two of the more recent examples.[30] Alexander VI (pope, 1492–1503), a native of Valencia and a member of the Spanish branch of the Borgia family, issued two bulls called Inter caetera, the first one dated May 3, 1493, and the second dated to the following day, May 4, but actually issued June 28 and predated. The first of these authorized the rulers of Spain to bring under their sway "countries and islands" discovered by Columbus, along with "their residents and inhabitants, and to bring them to the Catholic faith."[31] The second Inter caetera added to the terms of the first by drawing a line of demarcation "from the Arctic pole, namely to the north, to the Antarctic pole, namely to the south . . . the said line to be distant one hundred leagues towards the west and south of any of the islands commonly known as the Azores and Cape Verde," assigning to Spain the exclusive right to evangelize and trade in all lands to the west of that line not already under the control of a Christian prince.[32] Another bull, *Eximiae Devotionis,* was also dated May 3, but apparently did not become effective until July. It confirmed and made more explicit the grant of the newfound lands which had been conceded in the first *Inter caetera.*[33] The fourth and final bull relating to the New World issued that year by Alexander was *Dudum Siquidem,* dated September 26. It further extended and confirmed Spain's grant, giving her the right to exclude subjects of other crowns from those lands west of the line, and revoking earlier papal grants to Portugal that appeared to be in conflict with Spanish claims arising out of her discoveries. Neither bulls nor treaties, of course, could bind third parties, so that apart from the moral support they provided in terms of European international relations, it remained incumbent upon each of the nations involved to make good its claims.

The basis upon which Spain could assert these claims was laid out in the second *Inter caetera:*

> With this proviso, however that none of the islands and mainlands, found and to be found, discovered and to be discovered, beyond that said line towards the west and south, be in the actual possession of any Christian King or prince up to the birthday of our Lord Jesus Christ just past from which the present year one thousand four hundred and ninety three begins. And we make, appoint, and depute you and your said heirs and successors lords of them with full and free power, authority, and jurisdiction of every kind; with this proviso however, that by this our gift, grant, and assignment no right acquired by any Christian prince, who may be in actual possession of said islands and mainlands prior to the said birthday of our Lord Jesus Christ, is hereby to be understood to be withdrawn or taken away.[34]

The exact import of that wording was controversial at the time and has been much argued about ever since. At the time of the bulls, every Spaniard was said to have believed that the pope had granted Spain outright possession of her discoveries.[35] In ostensibly handing the New World over to Spain, was the pope exercising authority over Spanish temporal affairs, even if it was at the request of its monarchs? If that had been the case, why had Ferdinand and Isabella risked going to him in the first place, whether such an action was sanctioned by tradition or not? European monarchs — including those of Spain — were extremely jealous of their hard-won prerogatives, and would not have countenanced such a situation for a minute. The matter was, of course, much more complex and equivocal than such an explanation allows for, and smacked of opportunism on both sides. By obtaining papal sanction to take whatever measures would be necessary to evangelize the non-Christian inhabitants of the newfound lands, the Spanish monarchs bolstered their claim and at the same time acknowledged papal authority in spiritual matters. In this way pope and monarch recognized each other as supreme in their separate domains while upholding their own positions. Spain never allowed the pope to exercise direct authority in any of her colonies, either at the time of discovery or later. When Paul III attempted to do so in 1537 with his bull *Sublimis Deus Sic Dilexit* in defense of the rights of Amerindians, an attempt that was repeated by Urban VIII in 1639, Spanish authorities simply took care to see that the bulls were not proclaimed in their colonies. So, even as Spain sought to use papal authority to strengthen her position, and officially based her New World claims on the 1493 bulls, particularly the second *Inter caetera*,[36] she was careful to do this in conjunction with measures that were clearly within the temporal sphere: by invoking the rights of discovery; by negotiating demarcation lines with Portugal, such as those agreed upon in the Treaties of Tordesillas (1494) and Saragossa (1529); and by intimidation and the use of force.

The assumption in the bulls that Christians had the right to take control of the non-Christian New World was reinforced by the lifestyles of the first Amerindians encountered in the West Indies. They went naked as "their mothers bore them"[37] and were not organized into social, political, or religious institutions that Europeans could recognize. In the European view, the adoption of clothing symbolized the development of law, authority, and power; the lavishly dressed prince epitomized civility, whereas the naked Amerindian represented the state of nature.[38] This was the reason Columbus was taken aback when he was visited by an eighty-year-old cacique "who seemed respectable enough though he wore no clothes," and who furthermore displayed "sound judgment" despite his nudity.[39] Such observations were not enough to convince Europeans that peoples who habitually went naked, even on the most solemn occasions, were likely to possess social order or government, or were even capable of them, particularly when some were also reported to be cannibals. To Europeans, that was a clear violation of natural laws. Amerindians were quickly classed as "savages," not yet fully human although capable of becoming so, *ni roi, ni loi, ni foi*, according to the sixteenth-century catchphrase.[40] Life in "the manner of beasts in the woods" had an even more serious implication; it meant that New World peoples had no religion at all, and so could not even be classed as infidels.

Old World infidels, whose right to *dominium* and *imperium* Euro-

peans had been debating for so long, were socially and politically organized within hierarchical institutions, which, even if based on non-
Christian principles, were conceded to possess authority, despite arguments about its legitimacy. Coming to terms with such authority
involved theological and political considerations, but could be worked
out apart from actual warfare, even if that was not always realized
in practice. Amerindians, on the other hand, were viewed as being
in their cultural infancy, which meant they could not possess the same
rights as those who had attained the maturity of civility. These attitudes were given a particular urgency when Amerindians were observed wearing gold and pearls, and were soon found to possess silver,
but were not attaching to these items the value that Europeans did.
As Columbus pointedly observed in his report on his fourth voyage,
the "lands of this part of the world, which are now under your High-
nesses' sway, are richer and more extensive than those of any other
Christian power. . . ."[41]

As was readily foreseeable, the papal bulls of 1493 did not sit well
with other European monarchs, whose initial discontent ballooned into
outrage when the extent of the grants was realized. But the bulls had
placed the powerful weapons of tradition and official sanction in the
hands of Spain and Portugal, and those nations were prepared to use
them to whatever extent and by whatever means necessary to defend
their positions. This was particularly serious in the case of Spain, already well on her way to becoming the superpower of sixteenth-century
Europe. Of the two nations (France and England) who were most inclined to take up the challenge, France was initially in the better position for such an enterprise. Since a head-on confrontation overseas
would place too much at risk, not to mention being far too costly, the
French Crown cast around for other means of realizing its goals before undertaking direct territorial challenges. These are worth considering in some detail, as France stepped into the lists and became
the first of the European powers to openly defy the status quo initiated by the Alexandrine bulls.

The first way that presented itself developed out of France's bur-
geoning textile industry, for which red dye, very rare in Europe, was
much in demand.[42] Quickly taking advantage of the new source of
the dye presented by the brazilwood that flourished along Brazil's Atlantic coast, the French moved to form alliances with the Tupinambá-
Guaraní, in whose lands the best stands were found. Since this was
territory indisputably within the Portuguese zone of influence according to the papal bulls, the French at first did not waste their ener-

gies making territorial claims that would have been controversial at best. Instead, they invoked the principles of freedom of trade and freedom of the seas for right of access[43] and concentrated on cultivating Tupinambá-Guaraní as partners for the cutting and preparation of the dyewood for shipping to Europe. Since the Tupi were the original inhabitants, or at least were there when the Europeans arrived, the French argued that they had a right to be consulted and to have their wishes taken into account. The legal basis for this was expressed in the Roman legal maxim that had long since become established in canon law, *quod omnes tangit, ab omnibus approbetur* (that which touches all is to be approved by all).[44] Wondering loudly if the doctrine did not apply to Amerindians as well as to Europeans and other peoples of the world, the French set about cultivating alliances with Amerindians in those areas where they wished to establish themselves. They reinforced this approach by bringing delegations of Brazilians to France to be presented at court, where they formally requested French protection for their lands and people, and missionaries to instruct them in Christianity. Baptismal spectaculars were staged at court for some of these visitors, with the greatest nobles of the land standing in as godparents.[45] A favorite form of public pageant of the period, royal civic entries, came to include Amerindians (usually Brazilians) in the procession of captives who made their submission to the king. Such public proclamations of France's claimed right to evangelize and colonize in the New World were more successful in marshaling the French people's support for their Crown's projects than in convincing colonial rivals. The Portuguese were able to defeat eventual French attempts at colonizing in Brazil, and finally, to curtail French trading activities along its coast. But it took them more than a century to do so.

Fifteen years before their first attempt to settle in Brazil (1555–60), the French had made a similar effort in Canada on the Saint Lawrence (1540–43). They had done this because in that northern region, European territorial claims were poorly defined and therefore open to dispute. Unlike the situation with Brazil, it was not at all clear at first on which side of the dividing line Canada lay. The Portuguese, already active in the cod fisheries of the Grand Banks, inclined toward the view that at least the eastern portion of the land was theirs, and in the second decade of the sixteenth century they sought to back up this position by establishing a colony somewhere on the North Atlantic coast (generally believed to have been on Cape Breton Island, but no supporting archaeological evidence has been found). It was not much longer-lived than the first French attempt to settle in Brazil, but for different reasons. The Portuguese were not really interested in colonizing so far north when they already had more than enough projects in other regions. While they attached considerable importance to the exploitation of the fisheries, they could continue that activity without the encumbrance of colonization.[46] Spaniards shared this view in regard to their own claims, but with some reservation, as in addition to the fisheries, Spanish Basques were developing a profitable oil industry from the whale run in the Strait of Belle Isle and the walrus rookeries in the Gulf of Saint Lawrence. Then as now, oil was important for Europe, and the North Atlantic coast was proving to be a major source. Further complicating the scene, the activities of French Breton fishermen were acknowledged by cartographers, who regularly included "Tierra de los bretones," "C. del breton," or variations thereof in their maps of the region. In effect, the Bretons were considered to have been the discoverers of those coasts.

The uncertainties of the situation were such that in 1524 France was emboldened to challenge directly the papal demarcation by sending Giovanni de Verrazzano (ca. 1485–1528) to explore the North Atlantic coast. Ostensibly he was looking for a passage to the Orient, but he was also instructed "to go in search of new lands for this most serene crown of France."[47] Although a northwestern route to the Orient proved to be elusive for Verrazzano as for others, his accomplishment in ascertaining that Acadia in the north was connected by twenty-four hundred kilometers (fifteen hundred miles) of continuous coast to Florida to the south has been ranked in importance with Cabral's discovery of Brazil twenty-four years earlier. Verrazzano established beyond doubt that America was a continent distinct from Asia.[48] Unfortunately, his instructions for the voyage are lost, as is his official report to Francis I (reign, 1515–47). The principal evidence known to have survived consists of several copies of a letter draft that appears to have formed part of that report. On this fragmentary basis it has been argued that since the letter "mentions neither acts of taking possession nor territorial claims," Verrazzano did not have such a purpose in view, despite observations to the contrary by such a well-known colonizer as René Goulaine de Laudonnière (d.ca. 1572) and the Jesuit missionary Pierre Biard (1567/68–1622).[49] This argument ignores the fact that the explorer reported his discoveries in proprietary terms: "all the land we found was called Francesca after our Francis."[50] He then proceeded to name specific places, with an eye to gratifying the king: an island after his mother, a region after a royal duchy, a bay after the king's sister, and so on. Other important French personages were similarly honored; Verrazzano was not only claiming territory for France, he was seeking highly placed support for another voyage to those coasts. The argument against this interpretation also ignores reported official interest in the commercial prospects raised by the voyage, spurred by citizens eager to capitalize on them: "And we hope that S.M. will entrust him [Verrazzano] again with half a dozen good vessels and that he will return to the voyage."[51] In this he was successful, and four ships were repaired and equipped for what appears to have been conceived as a colonial enterprise. It was reported that he intended

> to persuade the Most Christian King to send to those regions a good number of people, to live in certain places of the foresaid coast, which have a temperate climate, a very fertile soil with very beautiful rivers and harbors suitable for any fleet; the inhabitants of which places would be the source of many good effects, among others that of bringing those rough and ignorant people to the divine worship and to our most holy faith and of showing them how to cultivate the land, by means of transporting some animals from our Europe to those most spacious fields.[52]

But European politics interfered. Francis I, realizing that his planned invasion of Italy would involve him in war with the Holy Roman Empire's Charles V on both land and sea, requisitioned Verrazzano's ships for that purpose, aborting the proposed voyage.[53] The French king had decided to pursue his challenge to Spain in Europe rather than in America.

Despite France's failure to capitalize on Verrazzano's achievements, other European powers apparently were disposed to recognize that they gave France a valid claim to the North Atlantic coast. This is evidenced by the speed with which cartographers adopted the explorer's nomenclature. Verrazzano's original map has not survived; what is presumed to be a copy, by his younger brother Girolamo, is dated 1529. But two years earlier, in 1527, Vesconte de Maggiolo (fl. 1504–49) had already availed himself of Verrazzano's findings for his beautifully executed world planisphere. His is the first map that has come down to us to label the coast north of Florida "Francesca."[54] The explorer's work is also reflected in the Robertus de Bailly globe of 1530, which closely follows the cartography of Girolamo.[55] Also worthy of note is an anonymous Portuguese map, ca. 1550, which shows six fleur-de-lys flags along the coast from Florida to Labrador, indicating some sort of recognition of a French claim to the territory, all the more remarkable because of Portugal's own claims.[56] Gastaldi labeled the northeastern region "La Nuova Francia," a name that had first been used by Girolamo de Verrazzano under the form "Nova Gallia," but in conjunction with the Yucatán.[57] That France had established a generally recognized claim is clear enough; what is not so clear is why Francis I, after authorizing Verrazzano's expedition, hesitated to follow up the opportunities it revealed. There appear to have been some French trading voyages in the Chesapeake Bay area, and perhaps along adjacent coasts, but that is all. The fact that by 1524 it had become perfectly clear that at least Florida and its adjacent coasts were on the Spanish side of the line may have been a factor.[58]

Still, Verrazzano's voyage clearly established the feasibility for France of acquiring an overseas empire, which fitted in nicely with Francis's dream of national aggrandizement. It gave him room to maneuver, particularly toward the north, where colonial land claims were even more vague in geographical terms. His explorers could set up crosses, a traditional means by which Europeans claimed unoccupied territories, but they could always say that these were simple navigation markers should other powers raise objections.[59] There is no evidence that Verrazzano used such markers, but Jacques Cartier did set up crosses in 1534 and again in 1535–36. That Spain was concerned about Cartier's activities is evidenced by the fact that she kept a watch on them, without, however, making overt moves to interfere.[60] Cartier is reported to have used the navigational marker explanation when a native headman, presumed to be Donnacona of Stadacona (a Laurentian Iroquois village on the site of Quebec City), objected to a cross he had erected.[61] Even at that early date, some observant Amerindians had a clear perception of the implications of such actions on the part of Europeans.

France's circumspection in this regard was motivated by concern about the reaction of her European rivals, rather than by commitment to the rights of Amerindians as such. In selecting Canada as the site of her first colonization attempt in the Americas, she relied upon the claims she had established during the Cartier voyages, as well as upon lack of Iberian interest in the north, and the fact that both Spain and Portugal were fully occupied with more immediately attractive colonization projects elsewhere. There had also been prospects of a lucrative fur trade with the Amerindians, but they were to be hardly more realized at that time than was the colony itself. Even disillusion with a failed project, however, did not dampen hopes for a happier outcome in the future. This was indicated in an inscription on the

Decelier world map of 1550: "As it is not possible to trade with the people of this country because of their aloofness and the intemperance of the land and small profits, they [the French] had returned to France and hoped to come back when it pleased the King."[62] That the king had every intention of pursuing the matter was soon evident. In 1550 Henry II commissioned geographer Guillaume Le Testu to map the New World, particularly those areas where France was trading, or perceived promising commercial prospects, such as Brazil and Canada. In his *Cosmographie universelle selon les navigateurs tant anciens que modernes* . . . (Le Havre, 1555), dedicated to the admiral of France, Le Testu illustrated Canada with the French lilies fluttering over it.[63] Interestingly enough, the Portuguese mapmaker Antonio Pereira in 1545 had also shown the fleur-de-lys flying in Canada, indicating French settlements (probably fishing stations).[64]

Variant circumstances in Brazil and Canada had led France to use different methods in each country to challenge the Alexandrine bulls. In the first case, she had concentrated on alliances with the natives rather than on territorial claims, a technique that brought substantial benefits from trade but which did not result in permanent colonies. In Canada, she sought first to establish a tentative territorial claim before sending out colonists to make her presence a *fait accompli*. Neither procedure involved recognition of aboriginal rights in principle, but it did involve a de facto accommodation. The French never wavered from their view that Amerindians as "hommes sauvages" were living metaphors for antisocial forces and that it was their duty to mitigate these forces through evangelization — *humaniser*, as it was usually put. The rights they recognized for Amerindians were those of the individual, not of the nation.

It was the Spaniards, with their passionate concern for the rights of man within the framework of law, who provided the theoretical case for aboriginal rights. When Spanish actions in the New World did not measure up to the high ideals that had been elaborated in scholastic thinking, Spanish denunciations created the public scandal out of which the Black Legend was born. Although the Dominican Bartolomé de Las Casas (1484–1566) was to become the personification of this campaign, his was not the only, or even the first, voice to be heard. The question of the Spanish right to colonize the New World, and the way in which it could be done legally, was under official consideration in Spain when the issue came to a head dramatically in Hispaniola in 1511. Dominican friar Antonio de Montesinos (1486?–ca. 1530), in collusion with his superior and fellow monks, preached a sermon on a Sunday in Advent that had been selected because of the importance of the members of the congregation who would be present. Montesinos lashed out at *encomienda* (forced labor) and the maltreatment of Amerindians that had begun unofficially in the days of Christopher Columbus and which was continuing officially under the governorship of his brother, Diego. "Tell me," demanded the friar, "by what justice do you keep these Indians in such a cruel and horrible servitude? On what authority have you waged a detestable war against these people, who dwelt quietly and peacefully in their own land? . . . Are these not men? Have they not rational souls? . . . Be certain that, in such a state as this, you can no more be saved than the Moors or Turks."[65] When the colonists protested, another denunciatory sermon followed. Montesinos and his fellow friars were silenced in 1512 by royal order as well as by an order from the superior of the Dominicans in Spain, but the issues of the rights of Amerindians and the legality of their conquest were not to be so summarily disposed of. Even as the friars were disciplined, the first Laws of Burgos were passed in 1512.

The situation that had so aroused Montesinos and his fellow Dominicans had developed as a result of the opinion generally accepted in Europe that New World peoples were "savage," that is, somewhere between humans and animals, and thus by nature fit for servitude. The consequences of that view had been formulated by a Scotsman who had no direct interest either in Spain or the New World. His concern was with matters of principle rather than with the realities of colonization; in any event, his comments were published the year before the sermon of Montesinos. John Major (1469–1550), the leading scholastic theologian in Paris in the early sixteenth century, was a conciliarist who held that the body of the faithful of the Church, properly represented in a general council, was superior to the supreme pontiff.[66] But he also held that the pope had been acting within his jurisdiction when he had authorized Spain to evangelize Amerindians, and he supported Spanish New World colonization as a means of achieving that end. Major did this, despite upholding the right of non-Christian societies to political dominion, because of reports that Amerindians lived according to nature, like animals. In their case, Major thought that Aristotle's doctrine of natural servitude, "that some men are by nature free and others servile," would apply, which meant that Amerindians did not qualify for *dominium*.[67] According to Parry, Major was the first to use this dictum of Aristotle's in connection with New World peoples.[68] That this occurred so quickly, and on a point of theoretical principle rather than as a consequence of actual contact, points to the difficulties Europeans immediately experienced in fitting the strange civilities of the Americas within their concept world order.

The charges of the Dominicans in Hispaniola pressured the Spanish court into speeding up the drafting of laws to regularize the situation in the Indies. Among the learned men assembled at Burgos to consider Spain's legal position in this regard was the Dominican Matías de Paz (1468/70–1519), professor of theology at the University of Salamanca. His treatise "De dominio regum Hispaniae super Indos" ("Concerning the Rule of the King of Spain over the Indies") was finished in 1512.[69] Matías, approaching the issue in the terms by which it had been argued in Europe since the thirteenth century, held that Christian princes could wage war against infidels, but only to spread the faith; if the infidels wished to learn about Christianity, their lands could not with justice be invaded or permanently taken over against their will. If they accepted an invitation to learn about Christianity, by implication they were also accepting the dominion of a Christian prince, who, however, did not have the right to enslave them. The appointment of such a prince must be authorized by the pope, and the people were not to be oppressed but could be required to provide certain services and pay certain taxes and levies as did citizens in all states, including Spain. If oppression occurred, then restitution should be made. The implication of all this, of course, was to justify Spanish colonial activities in the New World.

Juan López de Palacios Rubios (1450–1524), a member of the Council of Castile and a leading jurist, also had been asked for his opinion. Although he acknowledged the rights of non-Christians more clearly than Matías, like the Dominican he argued along lines that were closer to Hostiensis than to Innocent IV. Natural law applied to Amerindians as to any of God's creatures, and the fact that they were infidels did not in itself prevail over the fact that they were rational beings, and they had the right to property and control over their own affairs.[70] But Palacios Rubios did not see those rights as being absolute; they were valid only with the consent of the Church, once that institution was aware of Amerindians' existence.[71] Even then, they could be lost in war justly waged against them. Although he saw himself as being in sympathy toward them, Palacios Rubios considered that the refusal of Amerindians to recognize the superiority of the Christian church, or to listen to its missionaries (even though they could not be forced to become Christians), was cause for a just war. He drew the line at enslavement, however, despite the considerable support for Aristotle's dictum, including that of Major, which he cited.[72] Apparently he saw himself as acting in the interests of Amerindians when he was asked to put into legal form the procedures he deemed necessary to require them to submit peacefully to Spain in accordance with the 1493 bulls. This document, the *requerimiento* ("requirement"), was to be read to Amerindians before undertaking military action against them. While it has been much ridiculed, it was a serious attempt on the part of the Spanish Crown to observe its legal obligations. Certainly Palacios Rubios saw it in that light; when asked about it, he held that it would protect the legal rights of all concerned, if the proper forms were observed.[73] Its first recorded use was in Darien in 1514, and what may have been the last was in Chile in the mid-sixteenth century; it was not formally abandoned until 1573.[74]

As a consequence of this soul-searching, the Laws of Burgos were passed in 1512 and augmented (or "clarified") in 1513, legalizing but also modifying and regulating *encomienda*, a form of servitude that stopped just short of slavery. The system had not been invented to meet New World conditions, although it was there that it was adjusted into what would be its final form; it had been long in use in Spain.[75] Since Amerindians had been adjudged not worthy of freedom, the alternative was servitude. The fact that such an influential theologian as Major had already come to that conclusion on a theoretical basis, without ever having met an Amerindian, did nothing to discourage such thinking. It provided the ideological basis for the thirty-five ordinances that made up the Laws of Burgos, which assumed Spaniards' right to regulate Amerindian life to conform to their notions of Christian civility, and also, not least, to provide a labor force for the Spanish exploitation of New World resources. Regulating conditions of work in the mines was a principal preoccupation of the laws.[76] Spain's concern about the legality of her position in the New World was genuine enough, but it was entirely within the context of European law. Still, the mutual rights and obligations of *jus gentium*, binding upon all nations, applied in the New World "in the same way as the pre-political Law of Nature had been binding upon individuals when they were living in a state of nature."[77] Since the principles of natural law were seen as being common to all mankind, their universal application presumed a universally similar perception of what they were. Such a stand did not allow for the possibility that Amerindians might not share such perceptions, but might have very different views both about the law itself and its application.

At this early date, before she was aware of the existence of either the Mexican or Inca empires, Spain did not consider the possibility of Amerindians possessing sovereignty. But she did recognize that quite apart from their position under natural law, they had rights by the very fact that she was claiming some of them as subjects. Accordingly, Spain began inquiries and experiments to ascertain the capacity of Amerindians to live in the manner of Spaniards. Model villages were established in which selected Amerindians were to be supervised in their new life in the Spanish manner.[78] Their failure strengthened the argument for reducing Amerindians to enforced service in the forms of *encomienda* and *repartimiento* and for allowing them, at best, only limited proprietary rights.

By the time Dominican Francisco de Vitoria was delivering his lectures on Amerindian rights at the University of Salamanca in 1532, Spain had conquered the Mexican empire and was in the process of conquering that of the Inca in Péru. These peoples wore clothes and were politically organized in ways recognizable to Europeans, even though they found some aspects of the Amerindian systems strange. The conquest of these empires was justified on the grounds of violations of natural law: human sacrifice and cannibalism in the case of the Mexicans, tyranny and the deification of the Inca in that of the Peruvians.[79] According to Vitoria, it followed that Spain not only had a right, but a duty, to seize "the provinces and the sovereignty of the natives";[80] in his words, "it is immaterial that all the Indians assent to rules and sacrifices of this kind and do not wish the Spaniards to champion them, for herein they are not of such legal independence as to be able to consign themselves or their children to death."[81] Other grounds would be the prevention of Spaniards from preaching the gospel[82] and an attempt on the part of Amerindian princes to force Christian converts to return to idolatry.[83]

Alberico Gentili and Hugo Grotius were Protestants who in general used the humanist arguments that Vitoria had advanced. Gentili agreed with Vitoria and others "who say that the cause of the Spaniards is just when they make war upon the Indians, who practised abominable lewdness even with beasts, and who ate human flesh, slaying men for that purpose. For such sins are contrary to human nature. . . . And against such men . . . war is made as against brutes."[84] Grotius also concurred that breaking the laws of nature, such as eating human flesh, justified war: "the most just war is against savage beasts, the next against men who are like beasts."[85] Grotius, however, was writing about barbarians in general, and not Amerindians in particular. Gentili, considering personal responsibility in wars, found that Amerindians were no more blameless than anyone else "in fighting for their king when the latter made war unjustly." He also upheld European seizure of unoccupied lands "even though such lands belong to the sovereign of that territory" on the grounds "of the law of nature which abhors a vacuum." He observed, significantly enough, "is not almost all of the New World unoccupied?"[86] This is an early version of occupation as a claim to sovereignty, an argument which the English would later turn effectively against the Spaniards.[87]

By the seventeenth century religion had ceased to be central to the issue of sovereignty, which by that time was also being argued in humanist terms; but humanism was not necessarily more favorable to Amerindians than theology had been. Instead, it reinforced the perception of Amerindians as "savages" living outside of society, a perception which influenced Europeans into believing that they had at best only minimal rights. But imperial rivalries could make strange bedfellows, and so France, which considered herself the most civilized of nations, made alliances with Amerindians she considered savage, in order to invoke the principle of consent and so legitimate her New World claims. Later, during her colonial wars with Britain, she would disclaim responsibility for the actions of Amerindians fighting in her cause on the grounds that they were independent allies, and so not under her control. That approach opened up the way for the later claim that this was a form of recognition, and as such could be used to support the position that Amerindians had been acknowledged as sovereign during early encounters with Europeans, at least by implication. That this was far from what the absolute monarchs of France had in mind at the time became only too clear once they were successful in establishing colonies in Amerindian lands; at that point, there was no question in the mind of French officialdom that the laws of France applied to the natives as well as to the settlers. Aboriginal rights never were the subject of debate in France that they were in Spain. But in the final analysis, as far as the natives were concerned, there was little in the terms of international law to distinguish the French approach from the Spanish in the matter of Amerindian sovereignty.

NOTES

The research and writing of this essay was made possible by a grant from the Social Sciences and Humanities Research Council of Canada. Translations of the Latin texts cited in this paper were done by Dr. Nicholas Wickenden, University of Alberta, who was also most helpful with his advice and criticisms. I would also like to express my appreciation to Dr. D. C. Johnson, also of the University of Alberta, who read the manuscript with an observant and critical eye.

1. The irony of these concerns lies in the fact that Europe, far from challenging the legitimacy of the non-Christian Roman Empire, upheld it as a model, particularly as it was during the time of Augustus. See, for example, Dante's *De Monarchia*.

2. Kenneth J. Pennington, Jr., "Bartolomé de Las Casas and the Tradition of Medieval Law," *Church History* 39, no. 2 (1970): 160. A very good synthesis of the origins of European concepts that came into play in the Americas during the Age of Discovery is that of Silvio Zavala, *La filosofía política en la conquista de América* (Mexico City: Fondo de Cultura Económica, 1947). (In English, *The Political Philosophy of the Conquest of America*, trans. Teener Hall [Mexico City: Editorial Cultura, 1953], which is the edition cited here.) See also Robert Benson, "Medieval Canonistic Origins of the Debate on the Lawfulness of the Spanish Conquest," in *First Images of America: The Impact of the New World on the Old*, ed. Fredi Chiappelli, 2 vols. (Los Angeles: University of California, 1976), I, 327–34.

3. The text in full reads: ". . . possessiones et iurisdictiones licite sine peccato possunt esse apud infideles haec. enim. non tamen pro fidelibus, sed pro omni rationabili creatura facta sunt, ut est pradictum. ipse enim solem suum oriri facit super bonos. et malso. ipse etiam volatilia pascit, Matthei c. 5. circa fin. et 6. et propter hoc dicimus, non licet Papae, vel fidelibus, auferre sua, sive domnia, sive iurisdictiones infidelibus, quia sine peccato possident. . . ." (Innocent IV, *Commentaria in quinque libros decretalium* [Turin, 1581], ad 3.34.8, fol. 176va–vb. Cited by James Muldoon, "Extra Ecclesiam non est imperium: The Canonists and the Legitimacy of Secular Power," *Studia Gratiana* 9 [1966]: 573–74, n. 45.) My presentation of the positions of Innocent and Hostiensis is largely based on Muldoon.

4. ". . . sed et contra alios infidels, qui nunc tenent terram, in qua jurisdictionem habuerunt Christiani Principes, potest Papa iuste facere praeceptum, et constitutionem, quod non molestant Christianos iniuste, qui subsunt eorum iurisdictioni, immo quod plus est, potest eos eximere a iurisdictione eorum, et dominio in totum . . . si male tractarent Christianos, posset eos privare per sententian iurisdictione, et dominio, quod super eos habent, tamen magna causa debet esse, quod ad hoc veniat. debet. enim. Papa eos quantum potest sustinere, dummodo periculum non sit Christianis, nec grave scandalum generetur" (Innocent IV, *Commentaria in quinque libros*, fol. 177ra. Cited by Muldoon, "Extra Ecclesiam," p. 574, n. 47.)

5. A letter sometimes attributed to Innocent IV, *Eger cui levia*, takes a contrary position and denies the legitimacy of power outside the church. The attribution of this letter is doubtful (Muldoon, "Extra Ecclesiam," pp. 575–78. See also Benson, "Medieval Canonistic Origins," n. 12.) However, it should be noted that the capacity of medieval writers to contradict themselves has greatly complicated the task of sorting out their thinking. See Michael Wilks, *The Problem of Sovereignty in the Middle Ages* (Cambridge: The University Press, 1963), p. ix.

6. 1 Cor. 6:1–8, cited by Muldoon, "Extra Ecclesiam," pp. 570–71. This is a weak argument when one considers Paul's express recognition of the jurisdiction of Caesar (Acts 25:10–11) and implicitly that of infidel princes in general when he urged obedience to those in authority without mention of the religious factor (Rom. 13:1–7), as did Peter (1 Pt. 2:13–14, 18). See also Stanislaus F. Belch, *Paulus Vladimiri and His Doctrine Concerning International Law and Politics*, 2 vols. (The Hague: Mouton, 1965), I, 404.

7. J. N. Figgis, *Political Thought from Gerson to Grotius: 1414–1625* (New York: Harper, 1960), p. 21.

8. ". . . infideles, qui nec potestatem Ecclesiae Romanae nec dominium recognoscunt nec ei obediunt, indignos regno, principatu, jurisdictione, et omni dominio iudicamus" (*Super III Decretalium*, 1581, 128vb, no. 27, cited by Belch, *Paulus Vladimiri*, I, 393.)

9. ". . . unde constanter asserimus quod de iure infideles debent subici fidelibus. non econtra. . . . Concedimus tamen quod infideles qui dominium ecclesie recognoscunt sunt ab ecclesia tolerandi: quia nec ad fidem precise cogendi sunt. . . . Tales etiam possunt habere possessiones et colonos christianos; et etiam iurisdictionem ex tolerantia ecclesie" (Hostiensis, *Lectura quinque Decretalium*, 2 vols. [Paris, 1512], ad 3.34.8, fol. 124va. Cited by Muldoon, "Extra Ecclesiam," p. 578, n. 58.) Brian Tierney analyzes Hostiensis' thought in *Church Law and Constitutional Thought* (London: Variorium Reprints, 1977), pp. 368–72. See also Wilks, *Problem of Sovereignty*, p. 166.

10. ". . . Immo et si male tractent christianos potest eos, privare per sententiam iurisdictione et dominio quod super eos habent" (Hostiensis, *Lectura*, fol. 124va. Cited by Muldoon, "Extra Ecclesiam," p. 579, n. 59).

11. "Sed ubi Christiani sub dominio infidelium habitant quibus nec resistere possunt: necesse est quod patientiam habeant: et de facto ipsorum dominium recognoscant" (ibid., p. 579, n. 60).

12. J. A. Watt, "Hostiensis on *Per venerabilem:* the Role of the College of Cardinals," in Brian Tierney and Peter Linehan, eds., *Authority and Power* (Cambridge: The University Press, 1980), p. 104. There is some debate whether Hostiensis considered this plenitude of power to reside in the pope personally, or in the pope with the cardinals (Tierney and Linehan, eds., pp. 106–13).

13. Thomas Aquinas, *Treatise on Law* (Chicago: Henry Regnery, 1969), pp. 40–42.

14. F. S. Ruddy, "Origin and Development of the Concept of International Law," *Columbia Journal of Transnational Law* 7, no. 2 (1968): 235–38. See also Arthur Nussbaum, *A Concise History of the Law of Nations* (New York: Macmillan, 1954), p. 38.

15. Ruddy, "Concept of International Law," p. 239.

16. Arthur P. Monahan, *John of Paris on Royal and Papal Power* (New York: Columbia University Press, 1974), pp. 8–9.

17. Wilks, *Problem of Sovereignty*, pp. 92–105. Some have credited Vitoria with being the first jurist to reject the claims of the pope to exercise temporal power over rulers (for example, John H. Parry, *The Age of Reconnaissance* [New York: New American Library, 1964], p. 322). However, not only did John of Paris take up that position long before Vitoria, he was only one of several canonists to do so.

18. Walter Ullmann, *Law and Politics in the Middle Ages* (Ithaca and New York: Cornell University Press, 1975), pp. 282–83.

19. Walter Ullman, *A History of Political Thought: The Middle Ages* (Harmondsworth: Penguin, 1965), pp. 204–14; Ruddy, "Concept of International Law," p. 240. Ruddy holds that Machiavelli (1469–1527) carried Marsilius's ideas to their logical extreme in *The Prince*, in which he did away with the supreme authority of law without replacing it with anything (Ruddy, "Concept of International Law," p. 243).

20. Figgis, *Gerson to Grotius*, p. 47.

21. James Westfall Thompson and Edgar Nathaniel Johnson, *An Introduction to Medieval Europe 300–1500* (New York: W. W. Norton, 1937), pp. 848, 957–59.

22. Ullmann, *A History of Political Thought*, pp. 197–98. See also Wilks, *Problem of Sovereignty*, pp. 421–32.

23. Frederick H. Russell, "Paulus Vladimiri's Attack on the Just War: A Case Study of Legal Polemics," in Tierney and Linehan, eds., *Authority and Power*, p. 243; James Muldoon, "The Contribution of Medieval Canon Lawyers to the Formation of International Law," *Traditio* 28 (1972): 484.

24. Belch, *Paulus Vladimiri*, I, pp. 428–30, 460–63. This argument would later be supported by Hugo Grotius, *De jure belli ac pacis*, trans. Francis W. Kelsey (Washington, D.C.: Carnegie Institution, 1911; reprint, Bobbs-Merrill, 1925), bk. 2, ch. XX, s.XVIII, s.L, pp. 516–21. In the opinion of Grotius, neither could wars be waged justly against anyone because of error in interpreting divine law.

25. Russell, "Paulus Vladimiri's Attack," p. 244.

26. Ibid., p. 253. See also Nussbaum, *Law of Nations*, p. 38. Saint Thomas Aquinas held that three conditions were necessary for a war to be just: legal authority, just cause, and right intention (*Summa Theologia* IIa IIae, quest. XL, art.1.) In this he was following the thought of Saint Augustine (J. A. Fernandez-Santamaria, *The State, War and Peace. Spanish Political Thought in the Renaissance 1516–1559* [Cambridge: The University Press, 1977], p. 126ff.) See also Silvio Zavala, "The Doctrine of Just War" in Lewis Hanke, ed., *History of Latin American Civilization: The Colonial Experience* (Boston: Little, Brown, 1967), pp. 126–35. In 1680, almost three centuries after Vladimiri's arguments at Constance, Spain drew up the Recopilación de las Leyes de Indias, in which it was declared "that war cannot and must not be waged against the Indians of any province in order that they may receive the Holy Catholic Faith or give us obedience, or for any other cause whatsoever" (Collection of the Laws of the Indies, Law 9, bk III, ch. 4. Cited by Zavala, *Philosophy of the Conquest*, p. 36.)

27. Belch, *Paulus Vladimiri*, I, 412.

28. Ibid., I, 21.

29. Nussbaum (*Law of Nations*, p. 63) classifies this move as being of the supranational rather than the international plane.

30. Henry Folmer, *Franco-Spanish Rivalry in North America 1524–1763* (Glendale, Calif.: Arthur H. Clark, 1953), p. 20. Belch (*Paulus Vladimiri*, I, 89) maintains that the principle of distribution of infidel territories among Christian states for conquest began to be applied early in the fifteenth century, with Martin V (pope, 1417–31). In the case of the Canaries, the islands alternated between Castile and Portugal according to the currents of papal politics, until Spain obtained permanent control through the Treaty of Alcaçovas, 1479. In some ways, without pushing the comparison too far, the Spanish conquest of the Canaries can be seen as a precursor of that of the Americas. See Silvio Zavala, "Las conquistas de Canarias y América. Estudio comparativo," in *Estudios indianos* (Mexico City: Edición del Colegio Nacional, 1949), pp. 7–94.

31. Frances Gardiner Davenport, *European Treaties Bearing on the History of the United States and Its Dependencies to 1648* (Washington, D.C.: Carnegie Institution, 1917), p. 62. For a study of the bulls, see H. Vander Linden, "Alexander VI. and the Demarcation of the Maritime and Colonial Domains of Spain and Portugal, 1493–1494," *American Historical Review* 22, no. 1 (1916): 1–20; and Luis Weckmann-Muñoz, "The Alexandrine Bulls of 1493: Pseudo-Asiatic Documents," *First Images*, I, 201–209.

32. Davenport, *European Treaties*, pp. 77. The following year (1494) the Portuguese won Spain's agreement to move the line 270 leagues farther west, thus securing for Portugal the route to India and, as it turned out, to Brazil. In 1506 Pope Julius II confirmed this revised line in the bull *Ea Quae* (Davenport, *European Treaties*, pp.

84–100, 107–11; Parry, *Age of Reconnaissance*, pp. 168, 175). The Spanish view of the line is depicted in the *mappemonde* (1500) of Juan de la Cosa, owner and captain of the *Santa Maria*, who sailed with Columbus in 1493–94, and the Portuguese view in the Cantino chart (1502) (Leslie F. Hannon, *The Discoverers* [Toronto: McClelland and Stewart, 1971], pp. 65–67).

33. Davenport, *European Treaties*, p. 64.

34. Ibid., p. 77.

35. Lewis Hanke, *The Spanish Struggle for Justice in the Conquest of America* (Toronto: Little, Brown, 1965), p. 26.

36. Parry, *Age of Reconnaissance*, pp. 320–21; Vander Linden, "Alexander VI. and the Demarcation," pp. 15–18.

37. Those were Columbus's words, as recorded in his journal for 11–12 October 1492 (*The Journal of Christopher Columbus*, trans and ed. Sir Clements R. Markham [London: The Hakluyt Society, 1893], p. 38).

38. Olive Patricia Dickason, *The Myth of the Savage and the Beginnings of French Colonialism in the Americas* (Edmonton: University of Alberta Press, 1984), p. 50; Denys Hay, ed., *The Age of Renaissance* (London: Thames & Hudson, 1967), p. 335.

39. Pietro Martire d'Anghiera, *De Orbe Novo*, trans. and ed. Francis Augustus MacNutt, 2 vols. (New York: Putnam's, 1912), I, 102–103.

40. By the seventeenth century, the term "savage" was in general usage in French and English to designate Amerindians; Spanish and Portuguese used *indios*, which became hardly less pejorative. The Portuguese used *selvagens* to indicate nomadic hunters and gatherers, peoples whom the Spaniards referred to as *indios bravos*, or perhaps *indios barbaros*.

41. R. H. Major, trans. and ed. *Four Voyages to the New World: Letters and Selected Documents* (London: The Hakluyt Society, 1847; reprint, New York: Corinth Books, 1961), p. 201.

42. Fernand Braudel and Ernest Labrousse, *Histoire économique et sociale de la France*, 4 vols. (Paris: Presses universitaires de France, 1977–79), I, 246–54; Fernand Braudel, *La Méditerranée et le monde méditerranéen à l'époque du Philippe II* (Paris: Armand Colin), p. 167.

43. Both of these rights had long been seen as arising from natural law, that of freedom of the seas directly and that of trade indirectly though *jus gentium*. Vitoria would later use both of them to argue Spain's right to be in the New World (Francisco de Vitoria, *De Indis et de iure belli relectiones*, ed. Ernest Nys [Washington, D.C.: Smithsonian Institution, 1917], pp. 151–52).

44. This doctrine of consent had been very useful to such monarchs as Philip IV and Edward I in their struggles to establish national sovereignty. Concerning Edward, see Gaines Post, "A Romano-Canonical Maxim, 'Quod Omnes Tangit,' in Bracton," *Traditio* 4 (1946): 197–251.

45. Dickason, *Myth of the Savage*, pp. 213–17.

46. A 1525 map clearly places Labrador and Baccalaos (Newfoundland) and adjacent fishing grounds on the Portuguese side of the line. (Armando Cortesão and Aveline Teixeira da Mota, eds., *Portugaliae Monumenta Cartographica*, 6 vols. [Lisbon, 1960]. I: "Anónimo-Diogo Ribeiro," pl. 37; see also Lawrence C. Wroth, *The Voyages of Giovanni da Verrazzano 1524–1528* [New Haven, Conn.: Yale University Press, 1970], pl. 37.)

47. Wroth, *Verrazzano*, p. 142, and Carli letter, p. 157. Brian Slattery, "French Claims in North America, 1500–59," *Canadian Historical Review* 59, no. 2 (1978): 139–

69, makes a strong point of the fact that Verrazzano's primary purpose was to find a route to the Orient; however, that had been the primary purpose of all the voyages of exploration, including those of Columbus, Giovanni Caboto (John Cabot), the Corte Real brothers, and later, of Jacques Cartier. Even such late arrivals as Samuel de Champlain, who came to Canada early in the seventeenth century expressly to colonize, had not given up the idea of finding the elusive route.

48. Marcel Trudel, *Histoire de la Nouvelle-France I. Les vaines tentatives 1524–1603*. (Montreal: Fides, 1963), pp. 46–47, 49.

49. Slattery, "French Claims," pp. 141–42.

50. Wroth, *Verrazzano*, p. 159.

51. Ibid., Carli letter, p. 158.

52. Ibid., p. 264, citing Ramusio, *Navigationi et Viaggi III* (Venice, 1556), pp. 417–19.

53. Wroth, *Verrazzano*, pp. 160–62.

54. Ibid., pls. 19 and 22, and pp. 248–49.

55. William F. Ganong, *Crucial Maps* (Toronto: University of Toronto Press, 1964), p. 124.

56. Cortesão and Teixeira da Mota, *Portugaliae Monumenta*, I, pl. 80.

57. Ganong, *Crucial Maps*, pp. 105–106. Ganong examines the effects of Verrazzano's voyage on mapmakers in some detail (pp. 99–133). See also Wroth, *Verrazzano*, pp. 297–305, for a listing of primary and derivative maps.

58. In this connection it is interesting to note that France did not attempt to establish a colony on the Carolina coast until 1562, after the treaty of Cateau-Cambrésis, 1559, in which France and Spain had reached a verbal agreement that the actions of their nationals in the New World would not be considered a cause for war between the two countries in the Old.

59. As Slattery observes, "these royal symbols would clearly lend themselves to invocation in establishing a territorial claim, should this prove useful at some later stage" ("French Claims," p. 152).

60. H. P. Biggar, ed., *A Collection of Documents Relating to Jacques Cartier and the Sieur de Roberval* (Ottawa: Public Archives of Canada, 1930), pp. 447–67.

61. André Thevet, "Le Grand Insulaire et Pilotage," Bibliothèque Nationale, Paris, Département de Manuscrits, Fonds Français, MS 15452; François de Belleforest, *La cosmographie universelle de tout le monde*, 2 vols. (Paris: M. Sonnius, 1575), II, 2184; *The Voyages of Jacques Cartier*, ed. H. P. Biggar (Ottawa: Acland, 1924), pp. 66, 100.

62. Ganong, *Crucial Maps*, p. 363. "Et pource que Ilz na este possible (Avec les gentz dudict pays) faire trafique a raison de Leur austerite intemperance dudict pays et petit proffit sont retournes en France esperant y retourner quand il plaira au Roy."

63. Bibliothèque Nationale, Paris, map room, 87682. Illustrated in Hannon, *The Discoverers*, pp. 70–71.

64. Cortesão and Teixeira da Mota, *Portugaliae Monumenta* I, pl. 74.

65. Hanke, *The Spanish Struggle*, pp. 17–18. See also Bartolomé de Las Casas, *Historia a las Indias*, ed. Augustín Millares Carlo, 3 vols. (Mexico City: Fondo de Cultura Económica, 1951), bk. III, ch. IV. Begun in 1527 and worked on sporadically until the death of Las Casas in 1566, this manuscript was not published until 1875–76, in Madrid. See also Arthur Helps, *The Spanish Conquest in America*, 4 vols. (London: John Lane, 1900), I, 175–81. Today, a statue of Montesinos dominates the Santo Domingo harbor front.

66. Francis Oakley, "Almain and Major: Conciliar Theory on the Eve of the Reformation," *American Historical Review* 70, no. 3 (1965): 681–82. See also Francis Oakley,

"On the Road from Constance to 1688: The Political Thought of John Major and George Buchanan," *Journal of British Studies* 1, no. 2 (1962): 14-18.

67. John Major, *In Secundum Librum Sententiarum* (Paris, 1510), dist. 44, quest. 3.

68. John H. Parry, *The Spanish Theory of Empire in the Sixteenth Century* (Cambridge: The University Press, 1940), pp. 18-19; Zavala, *Political Philosophy of the Conquest*, pp. 45-46; Silvio Zavala, "Las doctrinas de Palacios Rubios y Matías de Paz ante la conquista de America," in *De las Islas del Mar Océano*, Juan López de Palacios Rubios (Mexico City: Fondo de Cultura Económica, 1954), pp. lxxxiv-lxxxv.

69. Hanke, *Spanish Struggle*, pp. 27-29; also, Vicente Beltrán de Heredia, "Un precursor del Maestro Vitoria, el P. Matías de Paz, O.P., y su tratado 'De dominio regnum Hispaniae super Indos," *La Ciencia Tomista* (1929): 3-20.

70. Zavala, ed., *De las Islas del Mar Océano*, ch. III, pp. 39-69.

71. Ibid., p. 69.

72. Ibid., p. 38.

73. Hanke, *Spanish Struggle*, p. 35.

74. An English translation of the document is in Helps, *Spanish Conquest*, I, 264-67, and in Lewis Hanke, "The 'Requerimiento' and Its Interpreters," *Revista de Historia de America* no. 1 (1938): 26-28. In its original form, it is in *Colección de documentos inéditos relativos al descubrimiento, conquista, y organización de las antiguas posesiones espãnoles de ultramar*, 25 vols. (Madrid, 1885-1932), XX, 311-14. By the end of the sixteenth century, doubts as to the legitimacy of colonial warfare in the Americas were becoming a chorus. For example, in 1594, Fray Alonso de Espinosa published *Del Origen y Milagros de la Santa Imagen de nuestra Señora de Candelaria* (Seville), in which he wrote: "It is an acknowledged fact, both as regards divine and human right, that the wars waged by the Spaniards against the natives of these islands (the Canaries), as well as against the Indians in the western regions, were unjust and without any reason to support them" (in English, *The Guanches of Tenerife*, trans. and ed. Sir Clements R. Markham [London: The Hakluyt Society, 1907], pp. 90-91).

75. Robert S. Chamberlain, "Simpson's *The Encomienda in New Spain* and Recent Encomienda Studies," *Hispanic American Historical Review* 34, no. 2 (1954): 238-50. See also Chamberlain's "The Pre-Conquest Tribute and Service System of the Maya as Preparation for the Spanish Repartimiento-Encomienda in Yucatan," *University of Miami Hispanic American Studies* no. 10 (1951).

76. Rafael Altamira, "El texto de las Leyes de Burgos de 1512," *Revista de Historia de América* no. 4 (1938): 5-79. Altamira also compares various versions of the laws, such as the one published in *Colección de documentos inéditos relativos al descubrimiento, conquista, y organización de las antiguas posesiones espãnoles de América y Oceanía*, 42 vols. (Madrid, 1864-84), I, 237-41, and as dealt with by Las Casas, *Historia de las Indias*, bk. III, ch. XV and XVI. An English version of the laws, by Roland D. Hussey of the University of California, Los Angeles, "Text of the Laws of Burgos: 1512-1513, Concerning the Treatment of the Indians," appeared in *Hispanic American Historical Review* 12, no. 3 (1932): 301-26.

77. Otto Gierke, *Natural Law and the Theory of Society 1500 to 1800*, trans. Ernest Barker (Boston: Beacon Press, 1957), p. 85. See also Parry, *Spanish Theory*, pp. 20-23.

78. These ventures are described by Hanke, *Spanish Struggle*, pp. 42-53.

79. See, for example, José de Acosta, *Histoire naturelle et moralle des Indes, tant Orientalles qu'Occidentalles*, trans. Robert Regnault (Paris, 1598), pp. 287v-88; Francisco López de Gómara, *Voyages et conquestes du Capitaine Ferdinand Courtois ès Indes Occidentalles*, trans. Guillaume le Breton (Paris, 1588), p. 28.

80. Vitoria, *De Indis*, III, 8.

81. Ibid., III, 15.

82. Ibid., III, 9, 12.

83. Ibid., III, 13.

84. Alberico Gentili, *De jure belli* (1612), trans. John C. Rolfe (Washington, D.C.: Carnegie Institution, 1933), bk. 1, ch. XXV, p. 122.

85. Grotius, *De jure belli ac pacis*, bk. 2, ch. X. s.XL, p. 506.

86. Gentili, *De jure belli*, bk. 1, ch. XXV, p. 126; ch. XVII, p. 81.

87. The Nootka controversy on the Canadian northwest coast, 1789–95, was Britain's first successful use of the doctrine of occupation as grounds for territorial claims against Spain. See Margaret A. Ormsby, *British Columbia: A History* (Vancouver: Macmillan, 1971), pp. 15–26; and Warren L. Cook, *Flood Tide of Empire* (New Haven, Conn.: Yale University Press, 1973), p. 136ff.

CORNELIUS J. JAENEN

Characteristics of French-Amerindian Contact in New France

THE FRENCH EXPERIENCE with the native peoples of New France, col-
lectively knows as Amerindians, seems to have been unique in the
annals of colonial history in a number of respects.[1] It differed sub-
stantially from the Anglo-American, the British, and the subsequent
American and Canadian national contacts. It differed even from the
French experience in Louisiana, the Antilles, and Guiana. While acknowledging that Western Europeans shared some common attitudes
and traditions, or a cultural baggage based on Classical and medieval
Christian concepts, and acknowledging that French relations with
native peoples were not wholly consistent when considered spatially
or temporally, we maintain basically the views expressed in *Friend
and Foe*, that the French experience was different from the Iberian
and Britannic contacts. The *sauvages*, a generally nonpejorative term
employed to designate the native peoples, were undoubtedly regarded
as inferior beings not on racial grounds but on sociocultural grounds.
Yet they were deemed capable of acquiring European *civility* and par-
taking of divine grace. *Francisation*, that virtually unattainable objective of total assimilation, would make of them the Frenchman's
equal. Our conviction remains, therefore, that Gary Nash's thesis (i.e.,
that the circumstances of colonization rather than nationalistic or religious differences accounted for the different policies pursued in the
Americas by the various European powers) fits New France.[2]

The belief that the French relationship was unique, or at least
notably different from the Anglo-American approach, was well established in French, British, and even Amerindian minds during the colonial period. In France, this conviction was canonized eventually in the
génie colonial thesis — the assertion that the French possessed a peculiar ability for getting along with native peoples, a national trait of
compatibility. In view of this supposedly inherent Gallic quality, France
seemed destined to assume a *mission civilisatrice* abroad. This interpretation also stressed the heavy-handed nature of Dutch and English

colonization, and the cruelties of the Portuguese and Spaniards. In the eighteenth century the French had rediscovered Las Casas and his indictment of the *conquistadores*, and had revived their sixteenth-century Black Legend charging the Spaniards with genocide, the systematic extermination of fifteen million to twenty million people. Even Voltaire recalled the first-hand description of Amerindians hunted down by fierce dogs and of natives hanged publicly in groups of thirteen. These nationalistic views, stressing the benign French approach to native peoples, were propagated by writers as diverse in background as the naturalist Buffon, the polemicist de Pauw, and the soldier Duret.[3]

In North America, Governor Vaudreuil opined that the southern tribes "prefer the French to all other nations." The missionary Charlevoix, who wrote a six-volume history of the colony in the 1740s, added that his nation was "the only one which has had the secret of winning the affection of the American natives." The trader Jérémie, who intruded into the regions claimed by the Hudson's Bay Company, found that the native hunting bands received the French as "brothers," but, said he, "they do not have the same attachment for the English." He was restating an affirmation made a generation earlier in Louisiana, where an officer remarked of the Amerindians that although the English of Carolina "appear richer and more liberal to them, yet they do not find their intercourse as pleasant as that of the French."[4] These sentiments confirm the sentiments of the native prophet who aroused Pontiac's supporters in 1763 against the Anglo-Americans, "these dogs dressed in red, who have come to rob you of your hunting grounds, and drive away the game." The Great Lakes tribes were asked to "take up the hatchet" against them, to "wipe them from the face of the earth," adding that "the children of your great father, the King of France, are not like the English," that they "love the red men," and even more improbable, "they understand the true mode of worshipping me," which referred to a revitalization movement. Another example is the Saulteaux chief who told the trader Alexander Henry in the autumn of 1761 that he knew that "our father, the king of France, is old and infirm" and tired of making war, so he had fallen asleep and consequently Canada had been conquered. But, he warned, "this slumber is drawing to a close. Already I hear our father waking up and asking about the fate of his children, the Indians."[5]

English commentaries at the time do not seem to have been in disagreement with these views. An observer in 1755 conceded that "the French have always had a great advantage over the English in treating with them." An anonymous pamphleteer specified that "according to their superior dexterity in address and civility of usage, they are more successful than we, in procuring and retaining their friendship." The clearest statement remains Thomas Mante's judgment in his *History of the Late War in North America* (1772):

> . . . and it must be owned, that the general behaviour of the French to the Indians was so very different from that of the English, as to give all the weight the French could wish to those lessons; the effects of which, accordingly, became every day more and more visible. We mention these particulars, not only to recommend the manner in which the French treat the Indians as highly deserving to be imitated by us; but to wear out the minds of such of our deluded countrymen as are not entirely destitute of good sense and humanity, the prejudice conceived against an innocent, much abused, and once happy people, who with all their simplicity, are no strangers to the first principles of morality; and, accordingly, entertain as deep a sense of the justice, benevolence, and condescension of their former friends, the French, as they do of the injustice, cruelty, and insolence, with which they have been used by their present fellow-subjects, the English.[6]

His appraisal attributed the French colonizing genius to an espousal of the myth of the *bon sauvage*, the Noble Savage of primitivist and Romantic literature, but also to an absence of the racism which marked the Anglo-Saxon contact.

The school of French imperial historians defined, canonized, and gave great prominence to this myth after 1870. Georges Hardy wrote that his countrymen "have been delivered more quickly of primitive expansionism and we have from the beginning incorporated with our needs of colonial domination the scruples of civilized peoples and the concern of educators." André Julien added that the "French had without argument a gift for conciliating the aborigines that no other people possessed to the same degree." Hubert Deschamps, in describing French colonial doctrines since the sixteenth century, stated that "their gift of sympathy [for the Amerindians], their facility of assimilation, their absence of racism were there from the beginning."[7]

The English-speaking world since Edmund Burke has generally adopted the same interpretation. No historian expressed the thesis more elegantly and succinctly than did the "Boston brahmin" Francis Parkman in the late nineteenth century: "Spanish civilization crushed the Indian; English civilization scorned and neglected him; French civilization embraced and cherished him." Philip Means, writing in the 1930s, commended the "singularly sympathetic and conciliating spirit which Frenchmen have always displayed toward races distinct from their own." Mason Wade, dean of Canadian studies in the United States, concluded that the French exemplified "a peculiar ability to conciliate aboriginal peoples" and win their confidence.[8]

Was this presumably felicitous relationship accompanied by positive, optimistic, and constructive assessments of native character and culture? Very early in the French contact experience a wide range of views emerged, among them contradictory evaluations even within the writings of a single author. Writers throughout Western Europe, including the few who had had firsthand experience in the New World, portrayed Amerindians according to the traditional philosophical concepts and intellectual constructs that were part of their cultural baggage and bias. There were optimistic assessments couched in the frameworks of the Golden Age, the Earthly Paradise, the Millennial Kingdom, the Lost Tribes of Israel, and Christian Utopianism; there were also pessimistic ones couched in the frameworks of the Chain of Being, the Monstrous World, Wild Men, and Satanic domination.[9] The emergence of positive themes such as the Noble Savage myth, the Four Stages theory, and the idea of inevitable progress and human perfectibility requires balancing with the emergence of negative themes such as colonial degeneration, the Vanishing Red Man thesis, figurism, and the infancy of the New World.

The Renaissance writers — Rabelais, Ronsard, and Montaigne — on the basis of travelers' tales, the gossip of fishermen in the port taverns, and glimpses of sometimes exotically bedecked Amerindian captives exhibited on public and religious occasions, set the pattern for an optimistic and romantic interpretation which passed into literature and history as the myth of the Noble Savage. Montaigne wrote: "Those people are wild, just as we call wild the fruits that Nature has produced by herself and in her normal course; whereas really it is those that we have changed artificially and led astray from the common order that we should rather call wild."[10] Montaigne initiated not only the concept of the natural man, unspoiled by social artificiality, but also indicated an effective and safe method of employing the New World and its cultures to criticize both church and state and both European man and European institutions.

Of equal antiquity and tenacity was the view of the Amerindian as a cruel, ferocious, subhuman, treacherous brute, and a cannibalistic savage. The savagery-civility dichotomy, which became implicit in so much of anthropological and historical writing, was explicitly and unashamedly present in many French assessments from the foundations of New France. In 1558 André Thévet described Amerindians as "a marvelously strange, wild and brutish people, without faith, without law, without religion and without any civilities" and "living like unreasoning beasts as nature had produced them, eating roots, men as well as women remaining ever naked, until perhaps such time as they will be frequented by Christians, from whom they will little by little learn to put off this brutishness to put on more civil and humane ways."[11] Savagery was defined as the absence of certain qualities and institutions. *Sauvages* were people devoid of civility, those possessing *ni foi, ni roi, ni loi,* as the popular expression phrased it. They were often seen as bestial, *homines sylvestris*, or the wild, hairy, naked, lustful, and dangerous beings who lived in the forests beyond the pale of organized life, fulfilling their animalistic instincts, while largely ignorant of God and morality. Jacques Cartier described them as "savage peoples living without a knowledge of God and the use of reason," and later Samuel de Champlain wrote of hostile tribes as "brute beasts having neither faith nor law, living without God and religion."[12]

Toward the end of the French régime in the Age of the Enlightenment the stereotype persisted. The great naturalist, the Comte de Buffon, gave the scientific assessment of America's native peoples as creatures that were barely human because they were still mired in *animalité*, subject to most natural phenomena, and were passive beings, almost inert peoples in static cultures in terms of dominating their environment. In his *Epoques de la Nature*, he generalized from the northern nomadic hunting bands for all Amerindians: ". . . having never brought into submission either the animals or the elements, having neither conquered the seas nor directed the course of rivers, nor cultivated the soil, he was in himself only an animal of the first order, and existed merely as a being of little consequence, a kind of powerless automation incapable of reforming or reinforcing nature."[13] Although Buffon believed, as did most of his contemporaries, that human nature was the same everywhere, he related racial or national differences to such factors as climate and environment, and consequently, to his consternation, he was cited as an authority on colonial degeneration.[14]

The theory of colonial degeneration received its clearest, most virulent and doctrinaire expression in the writings of Cornelius de Pauw. He argued that plants, animals, humans and possibly institutions inevitably degenerated when transplanted in the unfavorable American environment. Only snakes, insects, and harmful animals prospered. Amerindians were its natural inhabitants; consequently, they were idiot children, incurably lazy, and incapable of any mental progress. De

Pauw argued that physical degeneration was accompanied by moral and intellectual decline:

> . . . degeneration had attacked their senses and their organs: their soul had lost proportionately to the decline of their body. Nature having taken everything from one hemisphere of this globe in order to give it to the other, had placed in America only children, of whom it as yet had been unable to make men. When Europeans first reached the West Indies, in the fifteenth century, there was not a single American who could read or write: in our day there is still no American who can think. [15]

He undermined his own thesis somewhat through exaggeration, for even the most gullible French readers found it difficult to believe some Amerindians had pyramidal or conical craniums, and that many animals lost their tails and dogs their bark in America.

The abbé Raynal combined the degeneracy thesis with the figurist views of many of the Jesuit missionaries to arrive at his own interpretation. He relied heavily on the testimony of the missionary Joseph François Lafitau who saw the religion of the Iroquois among whom he labored as an imperfect survivor of an earlier universal revelation which God had given to primitive peoples and which was the foundation of a universal cultural unity. He wrote: "Everything points to some sickness from which the human race still suffers. The ruin of this world is still imprinted on the faces of its inhabitants; a race of men degraded and degenerate in their physical constitution, in their build, in their way of life, and in their minds which show so little aptitude for all the arts of civilization. . . ." [16] It was on the basis of such views that the religious in New France had concluded that the native peoples required tutors and executors because they were incapable of administering their own affairs.

The existence of eighteenth-century philosophical pessimism has often been obscured by the emphasis placed upon Enlightenment perfectibility, progress, cosmopolitanism, and rationalism. There has also been a widespread misunderstanding of Father Lafitau's and J. J. Rousseau's contributions to the myth of the noble savage. No single intellectual construct dominated the field and none was able to encompass the great diversity of views or to reflect the spectrum of interpretations. The discovery of America and the contact with "new men," according to some *philosophes*, may have been not only the most important event in European history but also the most disastrous. Many remained pessimistic about the value of colonial ventures and held very negative views about the virtue of colonized peoples.

The French relationship with the native peoples of New France was characterized, first of all, by a consistent, unitary, and centralized policy after Louis XIV assumed personal direction of his government in the metropole (1661) and in the colony (1663). It has sometimes been argued that New France was subject to arbitrary and despotic government, stifling metropolitan mercantilist economic controls, and burdensome clerical and seigneurial interference with personal liberty and innovation. Francis Parkman still casts a long shadow over the history of the French regime in North America. Yet, it can be demonstrated that a colonial government, located at the relatively isolated outpost of Quebec and functioning through correspondence with the Ministry of Marine, was more paternalistic than despotic. The Canadian colony held few attractions for settlers, little interest for investors, and limited opportunities for economic expansion. Of necessity, there was sensitivity to colonial and Amerindian interests as bureaucrats proceeded through consultations with local notables who were sensitive to regional and strategic issues. It can be argued that a traditional hierarchical society transplanted in the colony provided stability and order.[17]

Perhaps what is indicated as being a particular strength of the French relationship with the Amerindians is merely the reverse of the Anglo-American ineffectiveness, chaotic disunity, and inconsistency in dealing with the native peoples. Each British colony had its own particular policy, seldom in agreement with that of its neighbors, often at odds with trading partners, legislative assemblies, and land speculators, and nearly always in disagreement with imperial policies. Even after the defeat of Dieskau in 1755, Thomas Mante acknowledged the superiority of the French relationship: "These (Marine) troops, with the Canadians, who were as well, if not better qualified for service in that country, than the French regulars, joined to the numerous tribes of Indians in the French interest, being conducted by one chief, formed an infinitely more formidable power than the regular and provincial troops of the English, who could not unite their strength on account of the jarring interests of the different provinces."[18]

Amerindian affairs were within the jurisdiction of the governor-general in New France, who was also the chief military officer and the king's representative. Onontio (as the Amerindians called this man) spoke with authority, often commanded respect from friendly and unfriendly tribes alike, was careful to observe the protocol and even vocabulary associated with gift exchanges, formalization of alliances, and distribution of prisoners and booty; he represented a line of conduct applicable from Micmac and Abenakis country in the east to the Sioux and Cree country in the west. Generally, the tribes knew where they stood in their trade and warfare arrangements, and when there were shifts in French tactics and local practice, Canadian officers who commanded the scattered posts were instructed to explain how long-term strategy and alliances remained unchanged.[19] Missionaries were often influential in maintaining the "allied tribes" faithful to the French cause. Little distinction was made between the interests of the kingdom of France and those of the kingdom of God.

An important aspect of the consistent French policy was the avoidance of authoritarian overbearing and of pretension to rule the tribes of the upper country. A perceptive British observer reported in 1755 on the "secret," as he called it, of French influence among the Amerindians in comparison to the lack of British success: "They know too well the Spirit of the Indian Politics to affect a Superiority of Government over the Indians; Yet they have in Reality & Truth, of more solid Effect an Influence an Ascendency in all the Councils of all the Indians on the Continent and lead and direct their Measures, Not even Our Own Allies the Six Nations excepted."[20] Just as Versailles through its officials in the colony was sensitized to the limitations on the exercise of its authority and to the Canadian love of liberty, so the officials at Quebec, through the network of posts and mission stations manned by Marine soldiers, *congé* holders, and missionaries, were sensitized to the needs of the native peoples and the limitations on the exercise of French sovereignty. France exercised her sovereignty in North America through the independent Amerindian "nations": native self-government was the instrument of French power.

Another important characteristic of the French contact was the exploitation of the continent without extensive European occupation of the vast hinterland. Unlike the situation in the Anglo-American colonies, there was no westward-moving frontier of white settlement necessitating dispossession of the native peoples. New France was a collection of small seaboard colonies — Acadia, Isle Royale, and Louisiana — and the valley of the Saint Lawrence. The latter had been uninhabited when first visited by Cartier in the sixteenth century, but it had become a no-man's-land by the time Champlain built his *habitation* at Quebec in 1608 and the religious zealots founded Ville-Marie, that Christian utopian community on the strategic island of Montreal, in 1642. No natives were displaced to make room for French settlement in Canada, just as no Micmacs were displaced to make way for the implantation of Acadia.

There were posts in the interior with a small nucleus of French soldiers, Canadian farmers, and traders, at Detroit, Michilimackinac, and Kaskaskia, for example. But in 1664 the government forbade agricultural settlement up-country from Montreal and in 1716 refused to grant seigneuries in the region. There were two distinct regions, so to speak, in Canada: a riverine colony of French settlement where Amerindians were welcomed on designated seigneuries granted to missionaries and styled *réserves* or *réductions*, and the upper country or *pays d'en haut* comprising Amerindian ancestral lands where scattered missionaries, garrison troops, traders, and a few cultivators of corn, wheat, and tobacco benefited from natives' hospitality and sharing of land. The matters of discussion with the Amerindians revolved about fur trade issues, intertribal wars, the brandy traffic, and missionary activities and not, as in the cause of English contacts, about land cession, settlement, and treatment of captives.[21]

In recent historiography, it has become fashionable to portray the Amerindians as victims of European exploitation and as pawns in imperial rivalries and wars. This is a depiction which does little justice to Amerindian independence, initiative, and ability to exploit European involvement in the continent to native advantages. The French were unique perhaps in the sense that their experience in the hinterland or upper Canada quickly taught them that they were obliged in matters both of war and of trade to keep constantly in mind the Amerindian interests. Le Maire's memorandum of 1717 defined the situation succinctly:

> The Trade with the Indians is a necessary commerce; and even if the colonists were able to manage without it, the State is virtually forced to maintain it, if it wishes to maintain Peace, unless one wished to follow the cruel resolution of destroying all the Indians, which is contrary at once to both nature and Religion. There is no middle course; one must have the natives either as friend or foe; and whoever wants him as a friend, must furnish him with his necessities at conditions which allow him to procure them.[22]

The Intendant Raudot said that it was impossible to force French military or commercial policy on them: "We can only solicit them not to deal with the English and we can in no way prevent them from doing so." There was no question of coercion or threat in dealing with native peoples.

Nevertheless, it is true that Amerindians became increasingly dependent on European trade goods and services. Similarly, Frenchmen became dependent on Amerindian hospitality, support, and services. Neither party was able to extricate itself from this relationship, although there is evidence to indicate that there were times when each party would have welcomed such a course of action. A memorandum prepared for the Ministry of the Marine in 1730 reminded French bureaucrats of this North American reality: "It is agreed and it is a fact that generally all the natives like and fear the French, mistrust the English and believe all our goods to be superior; and they recognize that they cannot get along without our powder, without our white blankets, our cloth for over-clothing, our vermillion, cutlery, trinkets — so there are only yard-goods and kettles which they obtain more reasonable from the English and which are two items to which our attention must be turned. . . ."[23] The assertion made by Harold Innis in the *Fur Trade in Canada* (1930) and widely repeated, that English trade goods were of superior quality and more cheaply priced than French goods, seems questionable. It does not seem to have been the case along Hudson Bay, for example, because a factor of the Hudson's Bay Company wrote in 1728: "Never was any man so upbraided with our powder, kettles and hatchets, than we have been this summer by all the natives, especially by those that borders near the French."[24] This was by no means an isolated comment in the honorable London company's correspondence. There is abundant evidence that the Amerindians were astute traders who determined both the quality and quantity of goods they found acceptable. There are no reliable figures for the value of goods bartered in the upper country, but it is clear that the French enjoyed a preferred status throughout most of the period.

Thirdly, the French experience with aboriginal rights and title was quite different from the Anglo-American approach. It is often stated that the French never recognized any native entitlement. On the other hand, W. J. Eccles has contradicted this view and asserted that the French did recognize native sovereignty and never forced their dominion over the Amerindians.[25] The documentation would seem to indicate a position somewhere between these two extreme views. France did not formulate an explicit theory of aboriginal rights; she never treated with indigenous peoples for the surrender of their rights in the land; she never imposed her laws, never exacted tribute or taxes, and never imposed military obligations on the native peoples she considered to be under her protection and rule. But she did assert her sovereignty through the usual symbolic acts of taking possession of *terra nullius*, or lands not claimed and settled by another Christian prince. French dominion was proclaimed through the recognition of the independence of the "allied nations" who identified with the French in military, commercial, and missionary encounters.

Native concepts of property and of territory, whether horticultural plots or hunting territories, did not coincide with European legal concepts. Property was conceived by Europeans as being the basis of the social order; yet, during the Enlightenment, some theorists attacked its accumulation through inheritance and rank and regarded it as the basis for inequities. The abbé Pierre Dolivier, for example, went so far as to assert that "the earth belongs to all in common, and to no one in particular." Morelly, in his *Codes de la Nature* (1755), ranked in first place the precept that "nothing shall belong to anyone individually as his sole property, except such things as he puts to his personal use, whether for his needs, his pleasure, or his daily work."[26] These were views most Amerindians would have supported. They saw land as being no more the absolute possession of any individual than the air one breathed or the water on which one traveled.

That is not to say that Amerindians had no concept of possessory rights. The English traders had to obtain Iroquois permission to cross their territories to reach the Western tribes. The Montagnais granted right of passage across band territory, sometimes exacting a toll, in what anthropologists have called the hunting range system. The Montagnais were fearful that this right might not be respected when the five Postes du Roi passed to the British in 1760. They therefore instructed their missionary to appeal to the commander of the British occupation forces: "Our father, we learn that our lands are to be given away not only to trade thereon but also to give them in full title to various individuals. . . . We have always been a free nation, and now we will become slaves, which would be very difficult to accept after having enjoyed our liberty for so long."[27] The implication in this statement is that under French rule, even in the territory around Tadoussac, which had been reserved as the Postes du Roi and closed to colonization, the native peoples were free and independent.

In New France there was no alienation of Amerindian lands. Governor Courcelles' instructions in 1665 were that "all his adult subjects treat the Indians with kindness, justice and equity, never resorting to violence against them, nor will anyone take the lands on which they are living under the pretext that it would be better and more suitable if they were French."[28] There was no displacement of native population to make way for white European settlement; there was no advancing and threatening frontier of colonization. Instead, there were native peoples settled voluntarily within the French seigneurial tract in the Saint Lawrence valley on *réserves* administered by the missionary clergy, and there were also small islands of French settlement scattered at strategic commercial and military locations in the Amerindian hinterlands. The French, like other European powers, claimed sovereignty over the lands they "discovered" and employed symbolic acts such as planting crosses, nailing the king's coat of arms on trees, or burying inscribed lead plates to establish this claim against the claims of European rivals. La Vérendrye's son, for example, took possession of the lands west of the Mandans in March, 1743 by secretly burying a lead plate and then erecting a stone cairn, saying to the local inhabitants that he was doing so "in memory of our coming to their lands."[29]

It would seem that under French sovereignty, Amerindian nations were *nations* because these people were conceived of as an ethnic group specific to a particular geographical location; they were not *états* because they were not believed to be organized under sovereign governments possessing coercive powers, and therefore they were not among the diplomatically recognized international "family of nations."

The missionary Charlevoix said that, although they made war in the manner of barbarians, "it must however be allowed that in treaties of peace, and generally in all negotiations, they display such dexterity, address and elevation of soul, as would bring honour to the most civilized nations." Although they looked upon themselves "as the lords and sovereigns of the soil," they were "not so jealous of their property as to find fault with newcomers who settle on it, provided they do not attempt to molest them."[30] Hospitality and peaceful coexistence appeared to characterize the relationship, so long as dominance, coercion, and authoritarianism were avoided by the French.

The case of the Iroquois is an especially illuminating one because after 1713, by the terms of the Treaty of Utrecht, they theoretically came under British sovereignty. The French claimed that the Iroquois had made a formal submission to them in 1666, a fact reaffirmed by numerous *prises de possession*, but all the Five Nations themselves would concede was that they had extended hospitality and had promised that the French "would always be assured of a lodge among them" and that the missionary "would always find his mat to welcome him."[31] A memorandum on missions in 1712 stated:

It must seem that the Iroquois recognize no masters. And although the French have posted the coat of arms of France among them before and after the English posted those of England, they nevertheless recognize no domination. That is what they reiterated and tried to establish twice during two assemblies which they held in Montreal during the summer of the present year. To leave in perpetuity marks of their independence from both the English and the French, they had an act drawn up in proper form to which they put their signs and native hieroglyphs.[32]

The French exploited such sentiments against the British. The Ministry of Marine expressed great satisfaction with La Galissonnière's tactics in this respect: "These Indians claim to be and in effect are independent of all nations, and their lands incontestably belong to them." A military report on the boundaries of the colony, dated 1755, expressed the official French view: "The Savages in question are free and independent and there are none who may be termed subjects of one crown or the other. The declaration of the Treaty of Utrecht in this respect is erroneous and cannot alter the nature of things. . . . These native nations are governed only by themselves. . . ."[33]

The Micmacs were quite emphatic in their assertions to the French governor at Louisbourg when they challenged France's right to cede their lands to Britain by the Treaty of Utrecht (1713): "But learn from us that we are on this ground which you trod under foot and upon which you walk as the trees which you see have started to come forth from it. It is ours and nothing will ever be able to take it away from us or make us abandon it."[34] Governor St. Ovide replied that he knew well that "the lands on which I tread, you possess them from all time," and then added that "the King of France your Father never had the intention of taking them from you" but had ceded only his own rights to the British Crown. This was a fine distinction between French sovereignty and Amerindian possession and rights of usufruct.

The French position was based in good measure on their peculiar military relationship with the Amerindians. The Abenakis, for example, were essential to the defense of Canada, serving as a buffer between the two European areas of settlement. A memorandum to Versailles explained the situation in these terms:

1. that this nation is the sole bulwark against the English or Iroquois.
2. that if we do not agree or do not pretend to agree to their rights over the country which they occupy, never will we be able to engage them in any war for the defence of this same country which is the first line of defence of Canada.[35]

The French claim to the Great Lakes region, and to the loyalty of its tribes, was founded on the same distinction between French sovereignty and Amerindian possession and independence. A memorandum of 1755 explained the situation as follows. "In 1671, all the Peoples of the North, of the West and the South adopted the King of France as their Father and their Sovereign, and declared themselves to be his faithful subjects. M. de St. Lusson, sub-délégué general at Montreal, went to visit their coasts, received their hommage and took once more solemn possession of their country."[36] The French might interpret this as a quasi-feudal submission, but the Amerindians would see it as a formal declaration that they voluntarily became His Most Christian Majesty's children inasmuch as their traditional rights were being respected.

European powers by the eighteenth century had created two different treaty systems: a European treaty system, in which the powers dealt with each other as members of the "family of nations," and an extended treaty system, in which the imperialistic powers dealt with the rest of the world, particularly aboriginal peoples. The French in dealing with their European rivals did not operate on the same diplomatic level or sphere as when dealing with the Iroquois, Abenakis, or Ottawa.[37] Sovereignty and spheres of influence were emphasized in interactions with other nation-states, whereas native independence and self-rule were stressed in the context of North American coexistence. The genius of French policy was that there was no inherent contradiction perceived between these two positions. So long as French seigneurial grants were limited to the Laurentian lowlands and so long as post commandants in the interior were circumspect in their statements and actions when dealing with the "allied nations," France could assume responsibility under international law for both her colonists and the aboriginal people. Native nationhood was protected by French sovereignty; French sovereignty was exercised through native nationhood and self-determination.

Fourthly, the French system of reserves, as has already been suggested, was an important aspect of interracial relations. The reserves as originally perceived in 1637 were designed to assist in the integration of Amerindian and French populations. The objective was to attract nomadic hunting and food-gathering tribes to designated seigneuries administered by the missionaries with proximity to French colonists in order to introduce the Amerindians to a sedentary, disciplined, agricultural, and Catholic community life. At the outset the reserves were intertribal and included traditionalists as well as Catholic converts. The Jesuits operated the Sillery reserve near Quebec and Prairie de la Madeleine reserve near Montreal, while the Sulpician secular priests had a reserve near Ville-Marie called La Montagne. The lack of assimilation into French society, the slow pace of conversion, the evil influences of the nearby French settlements, and especially the ravages of the brandy traffic imposed some fundamental changes on the reserve system. The reserves tended to move away from close contact with French settlers and the chief towns; thus, Lorette replaced Sillery, Sault au Récollet and eventually Lac des Deux Montagnes replaced La Montagne, while Sault Saint Louis or Kahnawaké replaced Prairie de la Madeleine. Later reserves, such as the Abenakis reserves at Bécancour and Saint François and the Mississiquoi, la Présentation, and Saint Régis reserves were even farther removed from the centers of French population and acted as buffers along the frontier with the English colonies. The reserve became an institution of segregation, or at least of gradual acculturation in relative isolation from the towns and seigneuries of Canada.

The uniqueness of the French reserves is demonstrated in the motives various natives had for settling there or remaining on them when return to ancestral homelands was a viable alternative. The Hurons at Lorette were remnants of the four Huron nations that had once lived in the Georgian Bay region where the Récollets and Jesuits had started their utopian interior mission. They were originally refugees from the Iroquois invasion of Huronia. Similarly, some of the Abenakis who settled on reserves south of Trois-Rivières were refugees from New England expansion into their lands. Others, notably Iroquois converts, came to Sault Saint Louis or Lac des Deux Montagnes as refugees from persecution and discrimination in their traditionalist villages.

The Iroquois council at Sault Saint Louis told the governor in 1722: "The first and sole motive which made us quit our country and our families was Religion. We sought a place to make it secure among us and in imitation of our Missionaries we found no better place than near the French."[38] There were some, on the other hand, who fled to the safety of the reserve because they had been accused of witchcraft in their village; the missionaries received them willingly, saying that "the devil unwillingly becomes the occasion of the salvation of these wretched fugitives by making it less difficult for them to embrace Christianity."[39]

The reserves also augmented their members through adoption of prisoners. These might even include New Englanders, especially women and children, who not infrequently would refuse to return to their relatives when the French arranged prisoner-of-war exchanges and offered to redeem them from adoptive families on the reserve. A missionary at Kahnawaké reported as follows in 1741: "Our Indians are always at war with the Chicachas, and from time to time they bring in a good number of slaves; but instead of retaliating by burning them at the stake, they adopt them in the village, instruct them in the mysteries of religion, and by holy baptism place them in a way of reaching heaven."[40]

The reserves were not without economic attraction to some enterprising individuals and families. Gifts of food, clothing and arms were regularly distributed on the reserves, and when the services of canoemen, guides, and interpreters were needed, the French turned first to the reserves for assistance, which was well remunerated. At Sault Saint Louis and Lac des Deux Montagnes the illicit fur trade that developed between Montreal and Albany merchants, and which may have siphoned off about one-third of the peltries of New France between 1710 and the 1750s, was an important source of employment for the "domiciled savages."[41] The legal situation was that Amerindians could be stopped only from carrying furs to Albany and luxury and trade goods back from northern New York in the interest of Montreal merchants; the natives were free to trade in their own interest with anyone. The mission Iroquois were the principal intermediaries in this substantial Albany trade, and their missionaries were widely believed to support their initiative. Toward the end of the French regime the Montagnais and Hurons at Lorette turned to selling moccasins, snowshoes, sashes, fur caps and mittens, collars of porcupine quills, bows and arrows, and paddles at the Quebec market.

Satisfactory economic rewards tended to make loyal military allies. The domiciled tribes, as they were called, made up an important contingent in all of the chief French military expeditions. They participated not only in frontier raiding on English settlements but also in long-range expeditions such as the war against the Chickasaws in the Carolinas. During such campaigns, wives and families of warriors were fed and clothed by the French. The reserves became veritable military bases, which served as a buffer to protect the French and their domiciled Amerindians from surprise attacks from the south and also as liaison posts to maintain the neutrality of the neighboring tribes under British rule. The French found themselves obliged to maintain the reserves, at considerable and increasing costs, even after it became apparent that the initial objective of assimilation into a French life-style was proceeding very slowly.[42]

The reserves never made French-style peasants of the Amerindians. At Lac des Deux Montagnes, for example, the Nipissings and Algonkins, who were nomadic hunters, left their village to hunt each winter and they were soon joined by the Iroquois of the same reserve, who, though originally semisedentary horticulturalists, showed little more interest in farming. The proximity of the forest of the Laurentides was reassuring to the Lorette families who, although their raising of cows, wheat, and rye in addition to traditional maize, beans, pumpkins, and sunflowers had brought some progress in agricultural skills, they nevertheless still sold the produce of their hunting, trapping, and fishing at Quebec. The reserves, in short, were successful in that they permitted some continuation of the traditional occupations and skills.[43]

Finally, the French contact was important for the degree to which it promoted or accelerated evaluation and criticism of metropolitan French society. This critique culminated, in a sense, in the French Revolution. The Baron de Lahontan, who gave a soldier's view of the New World, had a fictional chieftain named Adario satirize the illogic of Catholic beliefs and the vices of European society. Similarly, Claude Buffier concocted a dialogue in which the artificiality and boredom of civilized life were stressed, while at the same time native life was portrayed as being free and happy. Maubert de Gouvest also, in his *Lettres Iroquoises*, had his fictitious Igli write from France to Alha in Iroquois country urging a critical reconsideration of the earlier favorable impression of the French. Alha was asked to consider whether "these men are worthy of the sublime idea which our illustrious Iroquois had formed of them" and was advised to assure the Iroquois that "they are themselves the Sages of the Earth."[44]

Jean-Jacques Rousseau has been associated widely, and somewhat erroneously, with the myth of the Noble Savage. Rousseau never suggested that Frenchmen should or could return to the Iroquois level of human society. Nevertheless, he gave one of the clearest statements of the thesis that self-perfection in the individual led to all manner of evil in the human species. He concluded: "The more one thinks about it, the more one finds that this state was the best for man. . . . The example of the savages, who have almost all been found at this point, seems to confirm that the human race was made to remain in it always; that this state is the veritable prime of the world; and that all subsequent progress has been in appearance so many steps toward the perfection of the individual and in fact toward the decrepitude of the species."[45] Grasset de Saint-Sauveur, on the basis of similar assessments, doubted very much that Frenchmen should persist in attempting to civilize the native peoples: "Such are the mores of a people too often calumniated by travelers; in the depths of his wilderness, the Amerindian is adroit, laborious, intelligent, virtuous, a faithful friend, good husband and good father. What would he be were philosophy to discipline his soul and manners? . . . Perhaps he might stand to lose: he would become disciplined (policé) but corrupted."[46] Even the missionary-traveler, Father P. F. X. de Charlevoix, conceded that the liberty which the Amerindians enjoyed compensated sufficiently for the deprivations and inconveniences that characterized their life-style. These were as much reflections on a Europe burdened with its own complexities, controls, and class divisions as they were statements that primitive peoples exhibited naturally many of the virtues civilized men sought to cultivate.

In refuting de Pauw's thesis of colonial degeneracy, Pierre Poivre attempted in 1772 to assess the predominant French impression of Amerindian societies. He wrote:

> It follows from all that I have said above, that the soil and terrain of America, far from being degenerated, are virgin and generally better than those of our hemisphere; that the natural and exotic products are good and abundant; that the prodigious quantity of animals and plants have kept men there for a longer period in a savage way of life, through the facility they have enjoyed in clothing and feeding themselves: that the savages are certainly inferior in intellect and in learning to Europeans; but that they possess no less good sense, or reason than they; and that they are generally as robust, as brave, and much happier.[47]

Such a statement is valuable to the historian in indicating both the understanding and the prejudice, the sympathy and the ignorance, of a well-informed man of the Age of the Enlightenment.

The purpose of this essay has been to set out some characteristics of the French contact with the Amerindian peoples in the period from first recorded contact to the end of French rule in North America, with special emphasis placed on the eighteenth century experiences. It does not come as a surprise that this experience played a role in the emergence of a theoretical framework for the social sciences concerned with native peoples, the concept of civilization, and the evolution of societies in a pattern sometimes called progress. It was in part out of the reported nature of North American native societies that Turgot conceived and formulated his Four Stages theory of progression from hunting and collecting economies through pastoralism to agricultural societies, and eventually to sophisticated commercial and industrial societies. Turgot's lectures in the late 1740s at the Sorbonne developed the thesis that human societies progressed through successive stages according to their mode of subsistence, not according to different modes of political organization or some other kind of "life cycle."[48] Algonkin society, accordingly, could be regarded as a living model of human society in the first stage of its development, while Iroquoian society was already more "progressive," an assessment with which the missionary Joseph François Lafitau would have agreed. This hypothesis that all mankind progressed through the four successive stages of development, with the "sauvage" being the most primitive, was adopted eventually by Lewis H. Morgan in his *Ancient Society*. Both Friedrich Engels and Karl Marx relied heavily on Morgan's assumption that social evolution was universal, unilinear, automatic, and progressive. This theory of social evolution, according to which no country can skip any important phase in its industrial development, was important in the formulation of the Marxist "mode of production" concept.

Our chief concern, however, is not to establish some direct linkage between contemporary social theory and the interpretations of early French contact with native peoples. One cannot help notice, nevertheless, the overwhelming Europocentric view of history and of the world that Frenchmen had. They placed themselves at the center of the universal stage and judged other societies by the measure of their own. Be that as it may, in the French experience in America one catches sight of another spirit as well, that of cosmopolitanism and humanitarianism. This spirit manifested itself eventually in the Declaration of the Rights of Man and in such acts as the abolition of slavery. The French seem to have believed in their *génie colonial*, although it may have been more imagined than real, and in doing so they espoused a benevolent universalism.

What also emerges from this overview is the dynamism and vitality of Amerindian cultures at the time of contact. The Amerindians were free and independent peoples, willing to adjust to new circumstances, and sufficiently dynamic to deflect certain intruding elements of European civility to their own advantage. European and Amerindian societies were very different, each having some positive things to learn from the other. Neither saw the other as its ideal; yet neither saw the other as worthless.

The French contact experience has relevance today. Aboriginal rights need to be understood in native terms as well as European juridical terms. Sovereignty can be conceived in national, regional, and local spheres, and native self-government is once more perceived as feasible. There are other more general characteristics that we have singled out which are equally relevant to our times. There remains a need for clear and consistent policies. More attention needs to be given to peaceful coexistence and to historic rights. There is still need for greater self-criticism and the acknowledgment that we are not at the apex of human development, but that we ourselves are, in the words of the early writers, only in the "infancy of the world."

NOTES

This essay is a revised version of public lectures given at the University of Delhi in December, 1983, Columbia University in February, 1984, and the University of Texas at Arlington in April, 1986.

1. The term *Amerindian* is an unambiguous and practical appellation, used in the same sense as one would use *European* or *African*, to refer to peoples of many different cultures, languages, and traditions who historically share a continent and are perceived by "outsiders" as sharing some common social, political, and intellectual attributes. *Native peoples* is the politically accepted term in Canada at the present time.

2. Cornelius J. Jaenen, *Friend and Foe. Aspects of French-Amerindian Cultural Contact in the Sixteenth and Seventeenth Centuries* (New York: Columbia University Press, 1976), pp. 190–97; Gary B. Nash, *Red, White and Black: The Peoples of Early America* (Englewood Cliffs, N.J.: Prentice-Hall, 1974), pp. 66–88.

3. Michèle Duchet, *Anthropologie et histoire au siècle des lumières* (Paris: François Maspero, 1971), pp. 194–99, 279; Cornelius de Pauw, *Recherches philosophiques sur les Américains* (Berlin: F. J. Decker, 1768), I, 55–56, 61–63; Sieur Duret, *Voyage de Marseille à Lima et dans les autres lieux des Indes Occidentales* (Paris: J. B. Coignard, 1720), pp. 261–62; Pierre Chaunu, "La légende noire antihispanique," *Revue de Psychologie des Peuples* (1969): 188–223. The tradition had been established in France as early as 1667 by the Dominican missionary Jean-Baptiste du Tertre, author of *Histoire générale des Antilles habitées par les Français,* 4 vols. (Paris: Thomas Jolly, 1667–71).

4. Huntington Library, Vaudreuil Papers, Letterbook I, Vaudreuil to Maurepas, June 1, 1744, p. 260; P. F. X. de Charlevoix, *Histoire et description générale de la Nouvelle-France, avec le Journal historique d'un voyage* (Paris: O. F. Griffart, 1744), p. vii; Public Archives of Canada (hereafter cited as PAC), MG 18, H-27, Félix Martin Papers, Description of Hudson Bay and Strait by Jérémie, p. 196; J. F. Bernard, *Relation de la Louisiane, et du Fleuve Mississippi* (Amsterdam: J. F. Bernard, 1720), p. 10.

5. Citations from Francis Parkman, *The Conspiracy of Pontiac* (New York: Macmillan, 1962), p. 169; Sylvie Vincent and Bernard Arcand, *L'Image de l'Amerindian dans les manuels scolaires du Québec* (Montreal: H. M. H., 1979), p. 188.

6. Anonymous, *The Expediency of Securing Our American Colonies* (Edinburgh: n.p., 1763), p. 57; Thomas Mante, *The History of the Late War in North America and*

the Islands of the West-Indies (London: Strahan and Cadell, 1772), p. 479. Professor Herman Merivale's lectures at Oxford on colonization in 1839-41, published in 1861, contained the following assessment of the French contact: "No other Europeans have ever displayed equal talents for conciliating savages, or, it must be added, for approximating to their usages and modes of life."

7. Georges Hardy, *Histoire de la colonisation française* (Paris: Payot, 1931), p. vii; André Julien, *Les voyages de découverts et des premiers établissements* (Paris: Presses universitaires de France, 1948), p. 182; Hubert Deschamps, *Les méthodes et les doctrines coloniales de la France* (Paris: Armand Colin, 1953), p. 16.

8. Francis Parkman, *The Jesuits in North America in the Seventeenth Century* (Toronto: George Morang, 1899), I, 131; Philip Means, *The Spanish Main: Focus of Envy, 1492-1700* (Reprint, New York, 1965), p. 197; Mason Wade, "The French and the Indians," in H. Peckham and C. Gibson, eds., *Attitudes of Colonial Powers toward the American Indian* (Salt Lake City: University of Utah Press, 1969), pp. 61-79.

9. Cornelius J. Jaenen, "L'image de l'Amérique," in Fernand Braudel, ed., *Le monde de Jacques Cartier* (Paris: Berger-Levrault, 1984), pp. 201-16; "Conceptual Frameworks for French Views of America and Amerindians," *French Colonial Studies*, no. 2 (1978): 1-22; and "L'Amérique vue par les Français aux XVIe et XVIIe siècles" *Rapports, XVe Congrès International des Sciences historiques* (Bucarest, 1980), II, 272-78. See also, Lewis Hanke, *Aristotle and the American Indians* (Bloomington: Indiana University Press, 1970), pp. 44-73, and *The Spanish Struggle for Justice in the Conquest of America* (Boston: Little, Brown, 1966), pp. 111-31.

10. Donald M. Frame, ed., *Montaigne's Essays and Selected Writings* (New York, 1963), p. 89.

11. André Thévet, *Les singularitéz de la France antarctique, autrement nommée Amérique* (Paris: n.p., 1557), p. 51.

12. Olive P. Dickason, "The Concept of *l'homme sauvage* and Early French Colonialism in the Americas," *Revue Française d'Histoire d'Outre-Mer* 63, no. 234 (1977): 5-32; Archives Municipales de Saint-Malo, Série HH, Carton I, MS 1; Samuel de Champlain, *Voyages et découvertes faites en la Nouvelle-France* (Paris, 1620), p. 1.

13. Cited in Michèle Duchet, *Anthropologie et histoire au siècle des lumières* (Paris: François Maspero, 1971), p. 246. The translation is mine.

14. Georges-Louis Leclerc, Comte de Buffon, *Oeuvres complètes* (Paris: Imprimerie Royale, 1767), XV, 445-6.

15. Cornelius de Pauw, *Recherches philosophiques sur les Américains* (Berlin: F. J. Decker, 1774), I, 35, 221; II, 102, 153-54.

16. Guillaume-Thomas-François Raynal, *Histoire philosophique et politique des établissements des Européens dans les deux Indes* (Paris: Amable, Coste, 1820-21), IX, 25. Cf. Arnold H. Rowbotham, "Jesuit Figurists and Eighteenth Century Religion," *Journal of the History of Ideas* 17, no. 4 (October, 1956); 482-83.

17. Guy Frégault, *La civilisation de la Nouvelle-France* (Montreal: Pascal, 1944), pp. 126, 134-36.

18. Mante, *History of the Late War in North America*, p. 56. For a full treatment of the subject, consult Harry M. Ward, *Unite or Die: Intercolony Relations, 1690-1763* (Port Washington, N.Y.: National University Publications, 1971).

19. La Chauvignerie to Saint-Pierre, February 10, 1754, in Fernand Grenier, ed., *Papiers Contrecoeur et autres documents* (Quebec: Presses universitaires Laval, 1952), pp. 100-101, gives a good account of such an occasion.

20. Stanley Pargellis, ed., *Military Affairs in North America, 1748–1765* (New York: Archon Books, 1969), Thomas Pownall's Consideration of 1755, p. 165.

21. Cornelius J. Jaenen, *The French Relationship with the Native Peoples of New France* (Ottawa: Indian and Northern Affairs, 1985), *passim*.

22. PAC, MG 7, A-2, I, Fond français, MS. 12105, Mémoire de Le Maire (1717), p. 83.

23. PAC, MG 4, C-2, III, Mémoire sur l'état présent du Canada (1730), p. 12.

24. Archives des Colonies (hereafter, AC) (Paris), Série C¹¹D, VI, Subercase to Minister, December 20, 1708, fols. 166–66v; H. G. Davies, ed., *Letters from Hudson Bay, 1703–40* (London: Hudson Bay Record Society, 1965), p. 136. For the recent debate on the views expressed by Harold A. Innis in *The Fur Trade in Canada: An Introduction to Canadian Economic History* (New Haven, Conn.: Yale University Press, 1930), see W. J. Eccles, "A Belated Review of Harold Adam Innis, *The Fur Trade in Canada*," *Canadian Historical Review* 60, no. 4 (1979): 419–41; Hugh M. Grant, "One Step Forward, Two Steps Back: Innis, Eccles, and the Canadian Fur Trade," *Canadian Historical Review* 62, no. 2 (1981): 304–22; W. J. Eccles, "A Response to Hugh M. Grant on Innis," *Canadian Historical Review* 62, no. 3 (1981): 323–29.

25. Robert J. Surtees, *The Original People* (Toronto: Holt, Rinehart, and Winston, 1974), p. 60. Bruce G. Trigger, *Natives and Newcomers* (Montreal and Kingston: McGill–Queen's University Press, 1985), pp. 330–31; Peter A. Cumming and Neil H. Mickenburg, *Native Rights in Canada* (Toronto: Indian-Eskimo Association of Canada, 1972), pp. 14–16; W. J. Eccles, "Sovereignty-Association, 1500–1783," *Canadian Historical Review* 65, no. 4 (1984): 475, 478, 505, 510.

26. Pierre Dolivier, *Essai sur la justice primitive* (Paris, 1972), p. 17; Morelly, cited in Paul Hazard, *European Thought in the Eighteenth Century* (Cleveland: World Publishing Company, 1967), p. 177.

27. Coquart to General Murray, March 12, 1765, in Lorenzo Angers, *Chicoutimi, Poste de Traite (1676–1856)* (Montreal: Editions Leméac, 1971), p. 60.

28. Cited in Cumming and Mickenburg, *Native Rights in Canada*, p. 79. It should be noted that most of the ideas about native land tenure are based on comparatively recent ethnographic studies, not on the original historical sources of the sixteenth to eighteenth centuries. See Ralph Linton, "Land Tenure in Aboriginal America," in O. Lafarge, ed., *The Changing Indian* (Norman: University of Oklahoma Press, 1943), pp. 53–54.

29. Pierre Margry, ed., *Découvertes et établissements des Français dans l'ouest et dans le sud de l'Amérique septentrionale*, vol. VI, *Journal de la Vérendrye (1743)* (Paris: Maisonneuve, 1888), p. 609.

30. P. F. X. de Charlevoix, *Journal of a Voyage to North-America* (Reprint, Ann Arbor, Mich.: University Microfilms, 1966), I, 380.

31. PAC, MG 1, Série C¹¹A, I, Extracts from Diverse Relations (1646–84), p. 427.

32. PAC, MG 1, Série C¹¹E, II, Memorandum on Establishment of Missions among the Iroquois (Nov. 12, 1712), pp. 27–28.

33. AC (Paris), Série B, LXXXIX, Rouillé to La Jonquière, May 4, 1749, fol. 67; PAC, MG 5, B-1 XXIV, Discussions on Limits of Canada (May 9, 1755), p. 354.

34. PAC, MG 18, E-29, Discourse of Saint Ovide, n.d., n.p.

35. PAC, MG 18, H-27, Félix Martin Papers, Memorandum on Acadia and the Abenakis, p. 235.

36. PAC, MG 4, C-1, I, article 14, I, no. 5, Rights of French Crown in Canada (1755), p. 33.

37. Dorothy V. Jones, *License for Empire* (Chicago: University of Chicago Press,

1982), pp. 5–20; Brian Slattery, "The Land Rights of Indigenous Canadian Peoples as Affected by the Crown's Acquisition of Their Territories," D. Phil. thesis, Oxford University, 1979, pp. 91–92.

38. PAC, MG 1, Série C¹¹A, CVI, Memorandum of the Missionaries of Sault Saint Louis (May 12, 1722), p. 113.

39. Nau to Bonin, October 2, 1735, in Arthur E. Jones, ed., *The Aulneau Collection, 1734–1745* (Montreal: St. Mary's College, 1893), p. 64.

40. Ibid., Nau to Mme. Aulneau, October 3, 1741, p. 140.

41. PAC, MG 1, Série C¹¹A, XXXIII, Vaudreuil and Bégon to Minister (November 12, 1712), p. 56; PAC, MG 1, Série F-3, X, pt. 1, King to Vaudreuil and Bégon (June 8, 1721), pp. 168–69.

42. PAC, MG 1, Série C¹¹A, XXXV, Bégon to Minister (September 25, 1715), pp. 273–75.

43. PAC, MG 18, K-5, Franquet Papers, II, Voyage from Quebec (1752), pp. 61–64.

44. Baron de Lahontan, *Conversations de l'auteur de ces voyages avec Adario sauvage distingué* (Montreal: Editions Elysée, 1974), *passim;* Claude Buffier, *Cours des sciences sur des principes nouveaux pour former le langage et le coeur dans l'usage ordinaire de la vie* (Paris: Imprimerie Royale, 1732), pp. 954–57; J. H. Maubert de Gouvest, *Les lettres iroquoises* (Reprint, Paris, 1962), p. 84.

45. Jean-Jacques Rousseau, *Second Discours* (Reprint, New York, 1964), pt. 2, p. 151.

46. Jacques Grasset de Saint-Sauveur, *Moeurs, loix et coutumes des sauvages du Canada* (Paris: Auteur, 1788), p. 8.

47. Pierre Poivre, *De l'Amérique et des Américains, observations curieuses du philosophe La Douceur* (Berlin: Samuel Pitra, 1772), p. 114.

48. G. Schelle, ed., *Oeuvres de Turgot* (Reprint, Paris, 1913), I, 255–74.

ELIZABETH A. H. JOHN

The Riddle of Mapmaker
Juan Pedro Walker

JUAN PEDRO WALKER is the most shadowy of figures in the history of
North American cartography. His trail of evidence is fragmentary and
his legacy of maps sparse. But the Walker puzzle is worth constructing
in order to understand a little-known phase in the mapping of the trans-
Mississippi West and particularly of Texas.

Walker's story illustrates the mapmaker's role in the *process* of discovery. Remember that the *event* of discovery—the initial drama of
finding lands or peoples hitherto unknown—only paves the way for
the continuing *process* of discovery. The most profound challenges lie
in the confrontation of unlike peoples, addressed in this volume by professors Quinn and Dickason. Still, if discovery is to be fruitful, the land
itself demands attention. Not only must it be explored, it must be
mapped in order to be known geographically and defined politically
in terms of ownership and citizenship.

Hence the importance of the mapmaker in the process of discovery. Most early explorers could make only crude sketchmaps, but such
raw data could then be compiled in maps drafted by cartographers,
and thus placed in the context of existing geographical knowledge. Succeeding maps would develop greater detail as later reports supplied
new data. But no area could be mapped with any precision until mea-
sured by surveyors, an onerous and costly business of skilled fieldwork,
rarely undertaken until issues of boundaries became urgent.

Such political urgencies shaped the career of Juan Pedro Walker
in the early nineteenth century. He was one of those rare mapmakers
whose accomplishments ran the gamut from pioneer fieldwork to scientific draftsmanship and broad compilation of data. But Walker's role
in the mapping of western North America has been obscure, even mysterious, because his maps were never published and few of his manuscript maps survive. He might have been forgotten altogether had not
two of his contemporaries cited Walker maps as sources of informa-

tion for their own published maps. But even those citations were more puzzling than informative.

The more widely circulated reference to Walker appeared with the important new map of North America that the prestigious Philadelphia map publisher, Henry Tanner, produced in 1822. In his "Geographical Memoir," a small brochure accompanying the map, Tanner warned that authentic data concerning Spain's former possessions of Mexico and Guatemala were so scarce that he had found it necessary to rely upon the "Map of New California" that Don Pedro Walker had drawn in 1810 by the order of the captain-general of the Internal Provinces. Tanner himself had little confidence in it, but it was "the only one relating to a region hitherto a blank on our maps, which bears any mark of authenticity." Thus Walker's information figured in the new Tanner map with a note of warning about its doubtful character.[1]

John Hamilton Robinson, whose "Map of Mexico, Louisiana, and the Missouri Territory" credited his delineation of the west coast to Walker, could have reassured Tanner about Walker's qualifications, had not Robinson himself died shortly after publishing his map in 1819.[2] He knew Walker to be a competent cartographer with access to all of the geographic information available to Spanish officials of the Internal Provinces. Robinson also knew that Walker had personally surveyed some of that Spanish territory and that he had first served the United States. Why, then, had Walker made his career with the Spaniards rather than the Americans?

John Walker was born on January 19, 1781, to an English father and a French mother in New Orleans, then the capital of Spanish Louisiana.[3] Thus the lad grew up trilingual, a great advantage in the complex arena of the lower Mississippi valley. By the 1790s, his father, Peter Walker, was a prominent resident of the Natchez district, closely associated with its Spanish governor, Manuel Gayoso de Lemos. Another member of the governor's circle was the Scottish-born planter, William Dunbar, a lively scientist in the style of Thomas Jefferson. Dunbar was the official surveyor of the Natchez district under the Spanish regime, and would continue in that post under the Americans.

Young John Walker, remarkably bright and industrious, engaged the sympathetic interest of both Dunbar and Governor Gayoso. The lad had just turned seventeen when, with Dunbar's recommendation, he obtained a job with the first scientific commission that the United States government sent to the lower Mississippi. A few weeks later, Governor Gayoso offered a comparable job with the Spanish counterpart, which John declined on grounds of prior commitment to the American commissioner. It was such an extraordinary opportunity for learning and public service that Gayoso wished his own son were old enough to participate.

In 1795, in the Treaty of San Lorenzo (Pinckney's Treaty), Spain and the United States agreed upon the thirty-first parallel as the boundary between their territories east of the Mississippi River. A joint boundary commission would locate and mark the line from the Mississippi to the Atlantic. President George Washington appointed as commissioner for the United States Andrew Ellicott, a native of Maryland then living in Philadelphia, the nation's temporary capital. Although a famously difficult personality, Ellicott was a scientist of considerable competence who had already proven himself as a surveyor on the Mason-Dixon line, the southwestern boundary of New York, and the District of Columbia.[4] He had revised L'Enfant's plan for the city of Washington and had published the first map of the District of Columbia. Perhaps Ellicott's experience in the swamplands of the federal district seemed a particular qualification for the southern boundary survey, but no one in Philadelphia comprehended the challenges that the Deep South held for surveyors.

Commissioner Ellicott sailed down the Ohio and Mississippi rivers, taking copious observations all the way to Natchez, where he arrived in February, 1797. With him traveled two young assistants: David G. Gillespie, who had studied applied mathematics at the University of North Carolina,[5] and Ellicott's son Andrew (called Andy), whose qualifications other than kinship remain obscure. Camping near Natchez, the party marked time through more than a year of political and diplomatic turmoil before their work could begin. Meanwhile, Ellicott developed a warm friendship with fellow scientist Dunbar and also a cordial relationship with Governor Gayoso and his circle, including Peter Walker, whom Ellicott grew to admire.

By April 18, 1798, when Ellicott finally started mapping his way down the Mississippi from Natchez to begin the boundary survey, seventeen-year-old John Walker had joined his crew as the third of the assistants whom Ellicott always called "my young gentlemen." Their first task was to locate Ellicott's permanent observation camp as close to the true line as possible. So began two years of grueling fieldwork with the common surveying compass and chain, during which the lads would more than earn the complimentary words with which the irascible commissioner always described them.[6]

Spain's commissioner was Ellicott's "old and worthy friend,"[7] Maj.

Map of lower Louisiana, undated, signed by Juan Pedro Walker. (The Historic New Orleans Collection, Museum/Research Center [1977.97], New Orleans)

Stephen Minor, another native of Maryland who was then prospering in the Spanish service; Spain's official surveyor was a native of the Canary Islands, Thomas Power, who had sometime lived in Philadelphia. But Spain's leading scientist in the initial, westernmost phase was a man named William Dunbar, who came down from his Natchez plantation for a few weeks to assist Ellicott in the astronomical observations upon which they would fix the location of the thirty-first parallel.

While Ellicott stuck to his base camp, observing the stars and calculating, Gillespie, Walker, and young Ellicott pursued "the active and laborious part of the business" through astonishingly difficult terrain.

> The first twenty miles thru which the line has to pass is perhaps the most fertile of any in the United States and at the same time the most impenetrable — it can only be explored by using the cane knife and hatchet — the whole face of the country is covered with strong canes which stand almost as close together as hemp stalks and are generally from 20 to 35 feet

high and matted together with various species of vines. The timber is
lofty and abundant and the hills short, steep, and numerous. Was it not
for the ingenuity and industry of the young gentlemen in my family (in
which they far surpass the Spanish party) we should make but a poor
figure during the hot months.[8]

Wilderness was not their only foe. Once the dreaded "sickly sea-
son" began in May, fever plagued the party, including Walker. The
penny-pinching federal government seemed another enemy to its commission; woefully inadequate congressional appropriations for the
survey meant crippling shortages of equipment and provisions, and
the survey personnel found that their stipends could hardly cover their
expenses in that area of "amazingly high living costs."[9] They envied
the Spanish party's superior outfit.

Amidst those trying circumstances, an acrimonious feud soon
erupted between Commissioner Ellicott and his second in command,
Thomas Freeman, whom President Washington had appointed official surveyor for the American team. In October, 1798, Ellicott expelled
Freeman from the camp for alleged "improper conduct," then made
David Gillespie surveyor pro tem. From then on Walker worked as chain
bearer under Gillespie's direction.[10] They became close friends, united
by common interests and shared hardships and perhaps by mutual an-
tipathy toward the often obnoxious Ellicott. Letters exchanged among
Walker, Gillespie, Freeman, and Minor indicate that they all derided
the overweening commissioner and his son.

But Ellicott was delighted with Walker, whom he praised as "a
young gentleman of fine talents" and "the life of our business."[11] In
fact, he picked the lad as a prospective son-in-law, to be taken home
for one of the Ellicott daughters.

No wonder the commissioner praised his young gentlemen's "judgement and activity, in constructing rafts, opening roads, and exploring
the country."[12] Much of the time they had no information about the
terrain, which was still largely unexplored, and the swamps between
the pine ridges often proved so deep that the crew had to go far out
of its way to cross them. Provisions grew ever more scarce and the
stinginess of the government allowance more galling. The men under
David Gillespie's direction consumed more provisions than they were
entitled to by law during the eighteen days that it took them to correct
the lines and erect the mounds of earth from the Pearl River to Thompson's Creek, and even so they were without meat for six days.[13] Gillespie's report crackled with indignation at the government's parsimony.

The farther east the line progressed, the more vigorous became the objections of Indians—Choctaws, Creeks, and Seminoles—who feared that the survey foreshadowed the taking of their lands. Although open hostilities never erupted, the threat of attack loomed much of the time, and angry tribesmen repeatedly crippled the party by stealing its horses and sometimes its equipment. In the spring of 1800, the commissioners simply gave up, taking their final observations on the Atlantic coast and leaving to southern surveyor Patrick Taggart the final ordeal of running the line across the Okefenokee Swamp from the mouth of the Flint River to the source of the Saint Marys.[14]

After completing and ratifying their report at Saint Marys in April, 1800, both the American and the Spanish contingents sailed for Philadelphia. The latter would return home by way of Pittsburgh, and Minor would visit Washington en route. Ellicott was sure that they were up to no good.[15] Over the two years of the survey he had increasingly criticized Spain's contingent, calling them lazy, incompetent, and totally untrustworthy, and charging that they had left all the work up to him.

The documentary results of the survey were indeed voluminous: a lengthy journal, including the report to the two nations, and some eighteen feet of charts and plans based upon "an infinite number of calculations."[16] Ellicott proposed to capitalize upon his labors by publishing the results as soon as possible. He enlisted his "young friend Walker" to help prepare the charts and plans for the projected two volumes, the second of which would contain a topographical account of the region with, according to Ellicott, "a greater number of astronomical observations than was ever made by any one person before in the same time similarly situated."

So, late in May, 1800, John Walker landed in Philadelphia, committed to work on Ellicott's project, at least through the summer. Whether he knew of Ellicott's hope that he would marry into the family, or how he felt about that, is unknown. Ellicott, grappling with financial straits, bustled about in the weeks after his return home. John himself soon ran out of money and felt very much alone, for his friend Gillespie had quickly headed homeward to North Carolina. Nineteen-year-old John longed for word of his family, as well as money and paternal advice.

Nevertheless, Walker used his time well. Soon after his arrival, he enrolled in the Philadelphia Academy, a forerunner of the University of Pennsylvania, where he studied mathematics and the English language.[17] Within four months he reported remarkable progress to his father:

> I have read as far as the third Book of Euclid and am complete master of Splines. I am at present studying Astronomy. I have went through Navigation and Surveying. In a couple of weeks I shall begin Algebra. I am the first in the first Class of a hundred and odd. . . . I have to get up very early every morning and learn 4 propositions in Euclid by breakfast, go to the Academy at 8, return at 12, back at 2 in the evening and out at 5 — what time I have in the evening I employ it reading Modern Europe.

But what of his future? So many possibilities beckoned in Philadelphia.

> I could get a Midshipman's commission in the Navy when I made myself completely acquainted with mathematics — or get into one of the first merchantman in this port where I could get the command of one in a few voyages. I have a great desire to see Great Britain and Indeed all the principal cities in Europe. If you disapprove of my going into the Navy or going on a merchantman with a view of following for a living you will at least let me go one trip to England. It will cost me nothing; on the contrary I could get very good wages as I will be acquainted with Navigating and taking lunar observations. I have a very great desire to see the world — that Island specially from which my dear Father came.[18]

His Walker family background loomed large in John's thoughts, now that his service with Ellicott had brought him to the region to which they had first emigrated from England. He wrote to his father's sister in London. He also visited the once fine mills, now sadly in decline, that the Walkers had owned on the Patapsco River in Maryland three decades past, before they moved to Louisiana. That was a sentimental detour on his school vacation journey to the new federal city of Washington, where he thought the Capitol and President's House the handsomest buildings he had ever seen, and the surrounding country the poorest of his experience, except the pine hills of Georgia.

What of the expected work for Ellicott? Apparently that was postponed through the summer while the erstwhile commissioner struggled with his own financial crisis. Having spent three years and eight months carrying out an important commission for his country under extraordinarily difficult circumstances, Ellicott could obtain from the Adams administration neither audience nor pay for himself or his party. Some of the difficulty stemmed from the government's recent hasty removal from Philadelphia to the new capital at Washington; some was due to the turbulent politics of the presidential election year. Probably it did not help that Ellicott was known to be a Republican and a scientific correspondent of Vice-President Jefferson, a fellow member of the American Philosophical Society. Ellicott was reduced to selling his books and instruments to support his large family. Autumn found him desperate to publish the results of his commission in order to raise some money.[19]

Now Walker buckled down to work under Ellicott's supervision. Given the dearth of cash on both sides of the arrangement, perhaps room and board in Ellicott's home figured in Walker's compensation. Whatever their arrangement, the work went well. By the end of January, 1801, progress with the maps was so great that Ellicott had only a little more work to do on them. Walker was then at work on the huge map — more than six feet square — which would be the principal cartographic product of the southern boundary survey.[20]

What recognition was Walker's work receiving and how well was he becoming acquainted with Philadelphia's lively scientific community? Certainly he came to the attention of the American Philosophical Society in September, 1800, when Ellicott submitted to that organization the "astronomical and miscellaneous observations made on the boundary between the United States and His Catholic Majesty." After praising William Dunbar's superior scientific attainments and his contribution to the work of the commission, Ellicott recognized the junior members: "To my assistants Messrs. Gillespie, Ellicott, Junr., and Walker, the former of whom acted as surveyor, I have likewise to acknowledge my obligations, for the promptitude with which they executed the orders they received, and the aid they gave me in making the observations."[21]

Given Walker's intimate knowledge of the Natchez area, his connection with Dunbar, and his recent experience with the boundary survey, surely some of the inquisitive Philadelphians sought his conversation. Occasions to meet the intellectual community were ample, thanks to frequent evening lectures presented by the Philosophical Society, the Peale Museum, and others. Ellicott, himself a regular attendant, must have encouraged Walker to make the most of those opportunities, unless the continuing financial pinch ruled them out.

By May, 1801, a year after his return to Philadelphia, Ellicott had yet to see a penny from the government. In June he lamented that he had been nearly ruined by public service; he had yet to receive more than half his pay, and he and his family were suffering great hardship, in which Walker presumably shared. How embittering, then, to learn that the grateful Spanish monarchy had not only praised its survey party, but had also given them a bonus of twenty-six thousand dollars to divide among themselves. In contrast, Gillespie had needed to borrow money to go home to North Carolina, and there was no end in sight for Ellicott's ordeal.[22]

In October, 1801, Ellicott announced to President Jefferson that his great map was finished:

> It comprehends the Mississippi from the mouth of the Ohio down to the Gulf of Mexico, the province of West Florida and the whole southern boundary of the United States, accompanied with thirty-two pages (in portfolio) of manuscript remarks on the navigation of the rivers, proper positions for military works, etc. I have endeavoured to make it interesting both as a geographical and national document. It cost me more than 40 days labour and I intended to hand it to you myself immediately on your return to Washington, but have been prevented by accepting an appointment under the state government.[23]

Ellicott forwarded the accompanying notes to Jefferson in November, but not until the end of the year could he find a bearer willing to convey the six-foot, two-inch tin map case to Washington from Lancaster, Pennsylvania.[24] In the accompanying letter, Ellicott explained that

> in examining the map it will be necessary to have reference to the manuscript explanation which was forwarded to the President some time ago. The south boundary will furnish a scale of British statute miles, and on the meridian of the mouth of the Ohio you will see a scale of geographical miles. Not having had leisure to take a copy of the map, I wish no person may be allowed that privilege before I have time to do it myself.

None of the correspondence about the completed map mentions Walker's work on it. Whether John's name appeared on the map is unknown; it burned in the Capitol during the unfriendly British visit to Washington in 1814.[25] If Walker remained until the project was finished, then he probably left in the fall of 1801, about the time that Ellicott moved to Pennsylvania's new capital, Lancaster, to work in the state land office. Clearly, the draftsman did not stay long enough to make a duplicate for Ellicott. But whenever Walker left, his subsequent work shows that he was well equipped to build on his work with Ellicott and to replicate at least part of it.

Walker could not have carried home to Natchez a very favorable impression of the new republic. Not only had its stinginess imposed grievous hardships on its survey party in the field, but the new Jefferson administration had been little more responsive than its predecessors to the financial plight of Ellicott and his subordinates. Unhappily, the political situation in the Mississippi Territory had grown just as discouraging as that which Walker had seen in Philadelphia. The Jefferson administration had replaced the Federalist governor, Win-

throp Sargent, with Republican William C. C. Claiborne. Dunbar was
so disgusted with the upstart faction that had gained control of the
Mississippi House of Delegates and so gloomy about the region's prospects under Republican leadership that he had withdrawn from all
government business. Stephen Minor was thinking of moving from
Natchez to Louisiana, so as to continue under Spanish government.
Worst of all, in 1802 Governor Claiborne abruptly dismissed Peter
Walker from his position as court clerk, where his competence in Spanish and intimate knowledge of the preceding regime had made him
invaluable to Governor Sargent.[26]

If young John Walker consulted his old mentor Dunbar about the
outlook under the American government, he found no encouragement
there. By the fall of 1801, Dunbar was grievously disappointed.

> I have been much pleased with the expectation that under a president
> who is a Philosopher and a person of general science, learning and the
> arts will be patronized, invention and discovery encouraged and rewarded,
> but the cry of economy by the votaries of your present government alarms
> me.—While other governments and even societies of private individuals
> reward at great expence invention & ingenuity in arts and manufactures
> and carry on discoveries to the most distant corners of the globe and into
> the interior of continents of perilous approach, not excepting our own
> frontiers, is it not a reproach to our country that Congress confines her
> views to the Customs and the excise? In short, her policy appears to me
> to be such as governs the actions of a self-interested individual.[27]

Given the lad's own discouraging experience of the American govern-
ment's treatment of those who served it, the dismay of his friends in
Natchez, and, above all, his father's victimization by the spoils sys-
tem, it is hardly surprising that John gave up on the United States.
He crossed the Mississippi to Spanish Louisiana to make his career as
Juan Pedro Walker. Surveying was in great demand around the post
of Concordia (now Vidalia, Louisiana), where another friend of the
Walker family, Capt. José Vidal, was commandant. By summer, 1802,
Juan Pedro was an officially recognized surveyor in that district; by
1803 he held the position of *ayudante agrimensor* of Concordia.[28]

Then opportunity beckoned from Texas, where the people of Nacogdoches were having great difficulty in completing the construction
of a new church. Juan Macfalen, a thirty-six-year-old farmer from
Virginia who had lived in Nacogdoches for five years, saw in their
predicament a possibility of profit.[29] During an errand to Louisiana
early in 1803, Macfalen apparently learned that young Walker possessed some of the building skills so lacking in Nacogdoches and per-

suaded him to join in a proposal to finish that church. The two men would contract to complete the job at their own expense by September if the parishioners of Nacogdoches would then pay them in tame horses. Such animals could fetch a handsome sum in Louisiana's nearly insatiable market. How could Macfalen and Walker have known that Commandant General Nemesio Salcedo had lately issued at Chihuahua a ban on the exportation of livestock from Texas to Louisiana?[30] That decree had not reached Nacogdoches by the time Juan Pedro rode in with Macfalen on the night of March 28, bearing a passport from José Vidal accrediting him as the *ayudante agrimensor* of Concordia.[31]

Their proposition could not have been more timely. There had lately arrived from San Antonio the governor's exasperated order to finish that church forthwith, with the ardor appropriate to the exalted purposes of the faith. But ardor for such exacting construction was nearly as scarce as the requisite skills and materials in a community plagued by incessant rain and sickness and perpetual struggle for livelihood. Within a fortnight the parishioners agreed to contribute one horse each, for a total of 150, so as to get on with their own work and still be assured of a speedy end to both the project and the nagging of Father José María Delgadillo. On April 12, the Nacogdoches commandant, Miguel Músquiz, approved their contract with Macfalen and Walker, giving Walker permission to go to the post of Rapides (now Alexandria, Louisiana) to fetch the necessary nails and to recruit laborers. He left at once, taking with him Pedro Ybarbo and six horses in order to bring back the necessities for the project.[32] Walker reported back to Nacogdoches on May 18, with five workers following a day after. On May 29, he headed back to Natchitoches to hire three more carpenters for the project, returning on June 6 with three employees.[33] By midsummer the work was well advanced.

Meanwhile, Commandant Músquiz had realized that the intent of Macfalen and Walker to market their 150 horses in Louisiana was incompatible with the new ban, and in May proposed a compromise. Having little other choice, the two contractors agreed to keep the horses in Texas for whatever use they could make of them there. That agreement anticipated, and thus effectively protected them against, the June 20 ruling by Commandant General Salcedo that their contract was illegal and work on the church must be suspended. Músquiz stalled compliance by citing the compromise and arguing that the project was much too far along to stop, due to Walker's trips to Rapides and Natchitoches on behalf of the enterprise and his importation of nine workmen.[34] Thanks to Músquiz, Walker came relatively unscathed through his first bout with the bureaucracy of the Internal Provinces of New Spain.

On August 30, 1803, just as Walker's task in Nacogdoches neared completion, stunning news arrived from Natchitoches: the United States had purchased Louisiana.[35] Louisianans had not been greatly exercised about the prospect of transfer from Spanish to French governance, which they had anticipated for many months, ever since the news that His Catholic Majesty had retroceded Louisiana to Napoleon in 1802. But the prospect of governance by the brash new republic of the United States, so alien in language, law, and custom, gravely alarmed most Louisianans.

Few could have reacted so swiftly and decisively as did Juan Pedro Walker. Within three days he sought permission to move to the Internal Provinces of New Spain, declaring himself a native of New Orleans who had never known any government other than that of Spain and now wished to leave Louisiana because of the pending transfer to the United States, a government repugnant to him. Forwarding the petition to the commandant general, newly arrived Commandant José Joaquín Ugarte recommended Walker as a bachelor of respectable circumstances whose breeding, education, and knowledge could make him particularly useful.[36]

The time was exactly ripe. With extraordinary speed, Commandant General Salcedo responded with permission for Walker to settle in Texas.[37] However, he asked that Walker be urged instead to move to Coahuila, and he alerted the governor of that province, Col. Antonio Cordero, to expect the promising young man.

Meanwhile, Juan Pedro made a quick trip back home to settle his affairs and say his good-byes. At Concordia, he found Captain Vidal penning a vehement warning to the commandant at Nacogdoches. It reflects the climate of opinion in which Walker's move occurred:

> Poor possessions of Mexico with the new state of things! America has acquired from France all of Louisiana, and if they arrive to take possession clear to the boundaries that divide this province from that, God help us! This is the most ambitious, restless, lawless, conniving, changeable, and turbulent of all the Governments in the Universe. I am so disgusted with hearing them that I can hardly wait to leave them behind me after fourteen years that I have contended with them. Undoubtedly there are very respectable good men among them, and in general their people are the most industrious known, but what good is that if their Government does not have the vigor and command that it ought to have to curb the rabble

in which that land so abounds? My experience with them is that rigorous treatment is the only just means of keeping them within proper bounds. Luckily, all those who live in Louisiana said they are very satisfied with the Spanish government and weep to be separated from it, despite the fact that there are among them some so malevolent that it would be dangerous were they ever again vassals of His Majesty. If you admit them all, you will see within two years the trouble that they cause. These people have the greatest ease in insinuating themselves, generally are educated people, and cover with their hypocrisy the venom in their hearts. They study particularly the character, habits, and customs of Spaniards, and based on that knowledge, make their schemes. They contain their emotions, reign in their conscience, and disguise their policies — in this way the Protestant passes as a good Catholic, and the Spy displays his love for the Spanish government.

If His Majesty does not garrison that cordon with considerable forces to make them fearful, you, Sirs, will find yourselves daily beset by these people. I understand that the new Commandant General is an excellent military man of the best training; thus we can hope that . . . the territories of our sovereign will be respected in that part of the world, and conserved as is very important to his Royal Crown.[38]

Vidal, departing for a year's leave in Spain, had no intention of returning to live in American Louisiana. He hoped for a grant of land in Nacogdoches to which his slaves and other chattels could be removed to await his return, a matter in which he sought young Walker's help. Juan Pedro promised to move his property to Texas for him and take care of his business until his return, and he carried Vidal's request back to Nacogdoches, arriving there on October 20. Vidal also entrusted him with urgent confidential dispatches about American mischief-makers heading for Texas, referring Commandant Ugarte to the bearer for fuller explanation.[39] Vidal's display of confidence in Walker could only have reinforced the favorable impression that the young man had already made in Nacogdoches.

But what confidence could Walker have in the situation to which he would move? Was he only reacting against the Americans, or did positive opportunities attract him to the Internal Provinces? Probably the latter. While he was at Nacogdoches, that post experienced two flurries of excitement over maps that showed how valuable his cartographic skills could be on the northern frontier of New Spain.

One of the two Zacatecan friars stationed at Nacogdoches was Father José María Puelles, who knew something of mapping. Undoubtedly Juan Pedro knew him, and not solely in connection with the church project; they probably traveled together when both set out from Nacogdoches on April 12, Father Puelles to seek medical treatment in Natchitoches and Juan Pedro to fetch men and materials for the church. Certainly, they returned from Natchitoches together on June 6.[40] Given their common scientific interests and the scarcity of educated men in the community, the two young men—Walker, then twenty-three, and Puelles, thirty-one—probably became friends.[41]

That summer Father Puelles received a letter from Thomas Power, requesting a map or maps of the Internal Provinces. Power, an old acquaintance of Walker from the time when both served on the Spanish-American boundary survey, had lately been appointed by the Marqués de Casa Calvo to survey the Texas-Louisiana boundary on behalf of Spain. He specifically asked Puelles about La Bahía and Béxar in Texas, the province of New Mexico, and the course of the Rio Grande from its source. Puelles prudently turned the letter over to the secular authorities. Commandant General Salcedo forbade him to give Power any maps but asked that the good father send to headquarters at Chihuahua any map that he might have.[42]

Construing Salcedo's request as a proposal that he begin mapping the provinces bordering Louisiana, Father Puelles replied that he would gladly do the job if he were furnished the proper instruments and arrangements were made for him to travel over the lands that Salcedo wished to have mapped. Meanwhile, he had already prepared for the commandant general a map of Texas and its boundaries, which left Nacogdoches with the October 23 mail, just three days after Juan Pedro's final return from Louisiana.[43] At the end of November Puelles sent Salcedo another map, this one of the San Antonio River and its settlements. The priest noted that no better ones had been done either by Spaniards or by foreigners, all of whom had got the details all wrong. He intended next to attempt a map of New Mexico and the entire course of the Rio Grande, notwithstanding his lack of direct knowledge of that terrain. Father Puelles was terribly disappointed to learn that Salcedo wished him only to draw maps of the territories that he knew best and not to bother with the rest, because it would be difficult to supply the needed instruments and unduly bothersome for him to tour New Mexico and the Rio Grande.[44]

Meanwhile, it became obvious that the vague international boundary endangered Spanish interests, now that the aggressive Americans owned Louisiana. On September 13 Salcedo instructed Ugarte, commandant of Nacogdoches, to permit no alteration in the boundary between Texas and Louisiana. But to Ugarte's consternation, the post archives held neither map nor other document attesting the dividing line, and local opinions on the matter varied. He begged his superiors for some instrument on which to base a stand, but neither San Antonio nor Chihuahua had such a document. Father Puelles, terribly concerned about exaggerated claims now emanating from Louisiana, urged painstaking investigation of its boundaries with New Mexico and Texas, lest false tales cost the Crown dearly.[45]

Walker, who witnessed at Nacogdoches both the late summer and the mid-autumn agitation about maps, had precisely the cartographic skills so desperately needed in the Internal Provinces. It appeared that he could capitalize upon his skills by honoring the commandant general's request that he locate in Coahuila rather than Texas. Perhaps his good friend, Captain Vidal, had already recommended a military career as the best avenue in New Spain for Juan Pedro's abilities and ambitions. Perhaps the clinching argument was made in Coahuila by Governor Cordero, one of the ablest and most highly regarded officers ever to serve on the northern frontier.

However the decision evolved, in Coahuila, on March 28, 1804, Juan Pedro Walker joined the Flying Company of San Carlos de Parras as a cadet, that is, a volunteer serving in expectation of a commission.[46] By autumn he was surveying and mapping the Rio Grande and the Rio Guadalupe in the company of a lieutenant and a hundred dragoons.[47] By the end of the year Commandant General Salcedo could hardly say enough in praise of Walker's knowledge, talent, conduct, application, and leadership, all of which he had demonstrated in faithful discharge of various assignments. So great was Walker's potential usefulness to the Royal Service that Salcedo seized the first opportunity to commission him, jumping him over a more senior cadet who would normally have been entitled to that vacancy.[48]

So, on January 15, 1805, Juan Pedro gained the rank of second alférez in the Presidial Company of Janos in northern Nueva Vizcaya. By the end of 1805, he had made two campaigns and several patrols against the enemies (presumably Apaches), serving with enough distinction to win some additional merit pay. The year-end summary of Janos Company on December 31, 1805, shows Second Alférez Don Pedro Walker as a twenty-five-year-old bachelor of noble rank, in robust health, brave, industrious, capable, and of good conduct.[49] His salary was 450 pesos per annum, he was being paid regularly, and he ended the year with a favorable balance of 53 pesos, which must have been a relief after his poverty with the Americans.

Better still, Juan Pedro's special talents won recognition during his

first year as a commissioned officer. He mapped the southern margin
of the formidable Bolsón de Mapimí in 1805. That April found him
posted to Chihuahua to instruct cadets; soon he was head of the small
military school. For the remaining three years of his membership in
the Janos Company, Walker usually served in Chihuahua, where he
was attached to the headquarters of Commandant General Salcedo.

There Walker blossomed as a mapmaker. The commandant general was scrambling for proof of Spain's territorial claims in the vast
reaches where Louisiana abutted the Internal Provinces. Not only from
the archives at headquarters but from every archive throughout the
commandancy general, Salcedo was gathering all documents of possible bearing upon the boundaries. He relied principally on friars in
the search for documents: such scholarly Zacatecans as Father Puelles
combing the Nacogdoches archive and Father José María Rojas, then
assigned to Chihuahua, sifting the much larger holdings of the archive
of the commandancy general.[50] The ultimate concern was maps, not
only those found in the archives, but new ones such as a cartographer
could compile from the materials turned up by Salcedo's search, and
from such current fieldwork as Walker's.

Once Juan Pedro reported for duty at Chihuahua in the spring
of 1805, creating those maps became his responsibility. The few surviving Walker maps include some made in that first year. By autumn
he had compiled a map showing the Spaniards' understanding of the
Red and Arkansas rivers from source to confluence with the Mississippi, and also the lands northward to the Missouri and beyond. Salcedo sent that one to Mexico City, then argued that its very existence
rendered superfluous the proposed American exploration of the Red
and Arkansas rivers.[51] In just six months the commandant's new cartographer had proven his usefulness to the crown.

But 1806 brought emergencies that interrupted Juan Pedro's work
at the drafting board. Along the undefined border between Texas
and Louisiana a series of untoward incidents threatened to spark a
war that neither power really wanted. Both Spain and the United
States increased their forces in the area. From Coahuila came Walker's
first outfit, the Flying Company of San Carlos de Parras, whose Capt.
Sebastian Rodríguez assumed the Nacogdoches command. Quickly realizing that difficulties of communication between Spanish and American personnel caused dangerous misunderstandings, Captain Rodríguez remembered former Cadet Walker, not only for his competence
in both languages, but for his knowledge of the Americans. In March,

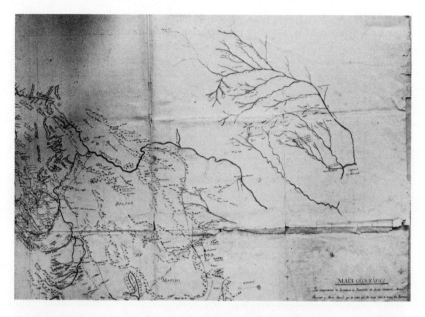

Juan Pedro Walker's 1805 draft map of the provinces of Texas, Coahuila, Nueva Vizcaya, and New Mexico. (Barker Texas History Center, University of Texas at Austin)

1806, Rodríguez urged his superiors to send Alférez Walker to Nacogdoches posthaste, on the grounds that his utmost usefulness to the Crown now would be on that volatile frontier.[52]

That argument prevailed. Although Rodríguez lost the Nacogdoches command only a fortnight after sending that request and reported back to San Antonio to face charges of exceeding his authority,[53] Juan Pedro did come to Nacogdoches sometime during the border crisis that dragged on into November. It seems most likely that he arrived in June with Col. Simón de Herrera, whose immediate responsibility was to check the American expedition that President Jefferson had sent, despite Spanish objections, to explore the Red River to its source.[54]

The American expedition started upstream from Natchitoches on June 2, 1806. Its leader was Thomas Freeman, whom Juan Pedro had known briefly as the controversial first surveyor with Ellicott's boundary commission.[55] Juan Pedro himself would surely have figured importantly in Freeman's new effort if only he had stayed in the United

States. In 1804, when Jefferson first contemplated exploration of the Red River, Walker and Gillespie were recommended to him as prospective scientists for the venture. The president then consulted Dunbar, who replied that Gillespie had the better education but that Walker was "perhaps superior in natural genius." Unfortunately, Walker was no longer available, having left Natchez and entered the Spanish service.[56]

Spanish authorities found it most expedient to intercept the American expedition a little way upstream from the old Caddo village on Red River. Colonel Herrera entrusted the delicate task to Ayudante Inspector Francisco Viana, who had lately taken command at Nacogdoches, and suggested that Father Puelles should accompany Viana's party. Colonel Cordero, then in San Antonio as acting governor of Texas, approved the idea and made the necessary arrangements with the religious authorities.[57] Unhappily, Father Puelles was not well enough to make the trip. But the map that he drew soon afterwards shows the course of that sector of the upper Red River and marks the place where the Americans turned back.[58] That map also shows up-to-date details of Louisiana, West Florida, and Mississippi Territory that Father Puelles probably could have obtained only from his friend Walker.

There is reason to conjecture that Juan Pedro accompanied Viana in the dual capacities of interpreter and geographer and that Puelles was invited to assist him in his observations and calculations. Given Juan Pedro's competence as a translator and his qualifications as a mapmaker, he was uniquely suited for that particular mission to the Red River. It seems unlikely that such competent leaders as Herrera and Cordero would have failed to exploit his abilities. Surviving versions — not, alas, the original — of Freeman's report of his July 28 encounter with Captain Viana's force name only three of the four Spanish officers; Viana's interpreter is mentioned, but not named.[59] Freeman, who relied on his own interpreter in talking with Viana, did not deal directly with Viana's man; after six years he could easily have failed to recognize his old acquaintance John Walker in Spanish uniform and with two years' depth of southwestern tan on his face.

Freeman bowed to Viana's courteous, but firm, demand to cease the unauthorized intrusion into Spanish territory and turned his party back downstream toward Natchitoches. Viana's party returned, triumphant, to Nacogdoches in August, just about the time that Governor Cordero himself arrived from San Antonio with still more troops.[60] The threat of war loomed over the border until November 6, when the Spanish and American commanders agreed to withdraw their troops

to the Sabine and the Arroyo Hondo respectively, leaving the interven-
ing territory neutral until diplomats could negotiate the boundary.

Oddly enough, Juan Pedro's presence became dispensable in late
October, just as the dangerous border confrontation approached its
climax. Governor Cordero authorized him to ride to the post of Orcoquisac, on the lower Trinity River, to take care of a debt that he had
there with Robert Tarpe. Cordero stipulated that Walker neither could
nor should remain at Orcoquisac, nor return to Nacogdoches; upon
concluding his business, he must proceed immediately to his assigned
post.[61] Tarpe was an Anglo-American carpenter, lately of Louisiana,
and the debt was probably a relic of Walker's church construction,
or of the disposition of the horses which he had collected as payment.[62]
But why was Walker excused from the Nacogdoches scene just as the
border crisis peaked? Did Cordero and Herrera learn of, and grow
uneasy about, Walker's acquaintance not only with Freeman but with
the principal American leaders in the mounting confrontation? Gen.
James Wilkinson and Col. Thomas Cushing were Walker family
friends.[63] Perhaps those American connections deepened official concern about Walker's inability to produce properly notarized proof of
his baptism, which was no trivial matter on that frontier.[64]

A more cheerful possibility is that cartographic considerations impelled Walker's speedy return to Chihuahua. His superiors would have
been eager for new maps incorporating any fieldwork accomplished
in the border region or further information gained from Puelles and
others at Nacogdoches. At the same time, the need for Walker as translator dwindled because Colonel Herrera, who negotiated directly with
the Americans in the final phase of the crisis, had an adequate command of English. Given those circumstances, it is hardly surprising
that Cordero hurried Juan Pedro back to Chihuahua; the wonder is
that he allowed the detour for personal business at Orcoquisac.

The spring of 1807 found Juan Pedro back in Chihuahua with his
new data, hard at work as a cartographer. On the walls of his quarters
hung maps of the various provinces, some of his own making, some
by others. But they all came down on April 2, to be stored in a cup-
board, so as not to be seen by the American who arrived that day.[65]

Walker's visitor was Lt. Zebulon Montgomery Pike, whom General Wilkinson had dispatched the previous summer from Saint Louis
on an expedition with formal instructions to find the headwaters of
the Arkansas and Red rivers and to woo Indians, particularly the Comanches. Not surprisingly, such errands took Pike into the northern
reaches of New Mexico, where he and his party, ostensibly lost, were

taken into custody as trespassers and escorted to Chihuahua to confront the commandant general. That created a great deal of work for Walker, whom Salcedo required not only to interpret all of the commandant's conversations with Pike, but to sort, transcribe, and translate Pike's numerous documents, and also to lodge Pike in his own quarters so that the American officer should have an English-speaking host.[66]

Although Pike suspected that the commandant general's real purpose was for Walker to spy upon him, the two young officers developed a cordial relationship, and on the whole Pike had a pleasant month's visit in Chihuahua. Walker told Pike something of his family background and gave various reasons for leaving the United States for the Spanish service, not the least of which was his father's shabby treatment by the Americans. He was dissatisfied with his low rank and claimed to have tendered his resignation, only to have it rejected because he was too useful. Walker did have an amazing array of duties besides his services to the commandant general and his headship at the small military academy. He was also involved professionally in the city's public waterworks, the building of a new church, and the manufacturing of arms.

Walker's manservant was an old black slave called Caesar, formerly of the Natchez area, who had been captured with the Philip Nolan party in Texas in 1801 and shipped with the other survivors to Chihuahua. Recognizing him as an old acquaintance from home, Juan Pedro arranged for Caesar to live with him. The garrulous servant proved very useful to Pike, not only informing him of Juan Pedro's maps but showing where they were stored. How closely Pike was able to study those maps and how much he learned by talking to Walker (and vice versa) is unknown. However, the map that Pike published in 1810 and that published by his companion, Dr. John Robinson, in 1819 indicate that both American explorers profited by seeing Walker's maps at Chihuahua.[67] In particular, Pike's map was the first ever published with reasonably accurate representation of the rivers of Texas, information that must have come from Juan Pedro.

The nature of the maps that Pike and Robinson might have seen in Walker's quarters can be deduced from the sparse inventory of his presently known works. Two, dated 1805, bear the signature Alférez of the Janos Presidial Company, Dn. Juan Pedro Walker. They include the provinces of Texas, Coahuila, Nueva Vizcaya, and Nuevo México, and were made at the direction of Commandant General Salcedo.

One of them (38 × 32 inches) is in the Huntington Library. A slightly variant one, in very fragile condition, is in the Barker Texas History Center at the University of Texas at Austin and is probably the one of which the Bancroft Library at the University of California, Berkeley, has the photocopy mentioned by Carl Wheat.[68] Labeled Phillipps Manuscript 29642, it was such an early acquisition that the Barker Center has no record of its provenance.

The Huntington Library version is one of several maps that Henry R. Wagner acquired with the papers that had belonged to Jean Louis Berlandier, a Swiss scientist who lived and worked in northeastern Mexico from 1826 to 1851.[69] Another of that group (22⅜ × 17 inches) is neither titled, dated, nor signed, but it is attributed — quite plausibly — to Walker, and has been thought also to date from about 1805. Wheat calls it "Nuevo-Mexico,"[70] but it is more descriptive to call it a map of the Comanchería. In it is compiled all available information about the Comanchería from the various documents held by the commandancy general, surely including the maps of Pedro Vial and his associates, and probably the report of the Amangual expedition as well. If the latter is the case, then the map would have been made after 1808, a little later than Wheat guessed.

Those are little more than rough drafts, which is probably why they remained in the northern Mexican borderlands. Walker's more polished maps were speedily forwarded to Mexico City and on to Spain, to meet the Crown's pressing need for maps to demonstrate its territorial claims. Of those, there are tantalizing traces. Sometime between May, 1807, and November, 1808, Salcedo sent to the viceroy a map — undoubtedly Walker's work — that displayed the boundary line and newly corrected directions of the Red, Arkansas, and Missouri rivers, contradicting the rendition of those streams on existing English and French maps. It also included the best available, though still not very satisfactory, rendition of the coast along the Gulf of Mexico. The site of Pike's forlorn little winter camp on the upper Rio Grande was marked as an American fort, which made that fleeting phenomenon look to officialdom in Mexico City and Spain much more threatening than the reality ever was. But that is a useful data point because it shows that the map was finished after Pike's visit to Chihuahua and therefore reflected the new information gleaned along the Texas-Louisiana border in 1806. Unfortunately, the original has yet to turn up; we have only its description in a letter from a Spanish officer who copied it at Mexico City for his superior in Spain, and his rather crude copy, now held by the Archivo Histórico Nacional in Madrid.[71]

Probably still to be found somewhere in Madrid is a signed Walker original of which only a photocopy is presently available.[72] The title translates as "Map of the Internal Provinces of Northeast, a portion of the Province of Louisiana: English possessions and little known country between 25 and 60 of latitude, formed with maps, diaries, and other evidence of journeys, campaigns and reconnaissances executed in large part by arrangement of Brig. Nemesio de Salcedo, Governor and Commandant General of the said Internal Provinces."

The scope of this map is much broader. On the east it runs from Hudson's Bay to New Orleans, and on the west from the Alaskan peninsula nearly to the tip of Baja California. Although the area westward from the front range of the Rocky Mountains to the Pacific Coast is a blank, labeled "unknown territory," the Missouri River system shows up in surprisingly good detail, even in a greatly reduced photocopy of dubious clarity.

The signature line reads: "Subteniente d. Juan Pedro Walker fecit, ano 1805," and the map seems to fit Salcedo's proud description of the one that he sent to Mexico City in the fall of 1805.[73] However, there is a puzzling discrepancy between the 1805 date and the title "subteniente," because it was not until September 19, 1808, that Juan Pedro Walker gained that rank.[74]

The promotion entailed transfer from the Janos Presidial Company to the Militia Corps of Mazatlán, but Walker still served in Chihuahua much of the time. Salcedo had been trying for more than a year to promote Juan Pedro in recognition of his accomplishments, and the change of units may simply have been a means of expediting promotion on a frontier where many officers awaited few vacancies in higher ranks. Another consideration may have been Walker's forty days of hospitalization during the first half of 1808;[75] a seaside city might have seemed a more suitable place for an ailing officer. But the transfer may also reflect Spain's growing concern about its western coastal frontier and consequent pressure to station a competent cartographer on the coast. A year later, in September, 1809, Walker rose to the rank of lieutenant in the same unit.

That chronology is important because it provides a time frame for the most recently discovered Walker map, now owned by The Historic New Orleans Collection. It is an untitled, undated manuscript map of southern Louisiana ($15\frac{1}{2} \times 21$ inches) in pen and ink with watercolor wash, signed "subteniente D. Juan Pedro Walker." That indicates that Walker produced it between September, 1808, and September, 1809, some five years after he left his native province, presumably relying upon data that he brought with him.

This is a much more polished product than the earlier ones, and shows signs of having been bound into a book. It displays more extensive detail, both human and topographical, than on any printed map of the area in that period. It shows ten Indian tribes and fifteen towns; the bayou system is portrayed in great detail, with extensive comment on some, and a large portion of the land to the west of the Mississippi is carefully shaded, apparently to indicate swampland or marsh. The remainder of the land surface is covered with miniature trees, hatchmarks to indicate savannas, etc. The thirty-first parallel is shown as the boundary of West Florida, and all of the details reflect Louisiana of 1803 as Walker had known it, with none of the changes that set in so rapidly after the American occupation.

It seems likely that the Louisiana map of ca. 1808 was one of a series covering the entire borderlands spectrum. The great challenge is to find the rest. The catalog of the Biblioteca Central Militar in Madrid lists several Internal Provinces maps with titles just such as Walker was producing in 1805–1808, and they date from that period. However, only one is shown to have been signed by him, the missing one represented by the 1969 photocopy. A few of the others are also missing. A few of the unsigned ones now available may be Walker's work; no conclusive identification can be made just by comparing slides of those with slides of known Walker works, and no comparison of originals has yet been possible. There is hope that some of the currently missing maps listed in the catalog, and others now quite unknown, will turn up in the course of the ambitious research on Spanish activity in the New World with which Spain will commemorate the Columbian Quincentenary.

What of the Walker maps made for the viceroy? The only one located thus far is in Mexico City, at the Archivo General de la Nación, where it is assumed to have been made in 1806–1809.[76] Entitled "Derrotero del Viaje que hizo el Marqués de San Miguel de Aguayo en el año de 1722," it is a tidy little ink drawing with some color wash, now splotchy from water damage, that Walker drafted from documents that Salcedo assembled to prove Spain's priority in Texas. It shows Aguayo's route from San Antonio to Los Adaes and from Presidio de la Bahía to San Antonio, with little detail that is not immediately germane to the Aguayo trek. It is signed "Ayudante Mayor Don Juan Pedro Walker."

That title also occurs with Walker's certification of a group of forty-six documents that he translated from English into Spanish for the commandant general. In that document, signed at Chihuahua, April 18, 1810, he identifies himself as Don Juan Pedro Walker, Teni-

ente de Caballeria y Ayudante Mayor del Cuerpo de Milicias de Mazatlán.[77] So it appears that Walker finished the map of the Aguayo
route after September, 1809, when he became a lieutenant at Mazatlán.

Lieutenant Walker was still *ayudante mayor* of the Mazatlán militia in 1811, when he was jailed at Chihuahua as a partisan of Father
Hidalgo's independence movement, which seems out of character for
Juan Pedro. No primary sources have emerged. Two reputable Mexican reference works offer conflicting versions. The first states that
Walker took arms as soon as Father Hidalgo declared for independence
in September, 1810, and followed his campaigns until captured in the
decisive battle of Acatita de Baján in March, 1811. This version has
Walker taken to Chihuahua, judged and sentenced to prison, then confined nearby at Encinillas, Nueva Vizcaya.[78] The second, more persuasive version identifies Walker as a retired lieutenant and *ayudante
mayor* of the militia of Mazatlán whom the authorities detained in
February, 1811, under suspicion as a partisan of the independence movement, holding him in the jail at Chihuahua until July 5.[79] The idea
that he was retired, at least temporarily, is not implausible in light
of his long hospitalization in 1808.

Whatever the truth or the extent of Walker's involvement with the
insurgents or the length of his incarceration, by January, 1813, he was
back at San Carlos, his first station in the Internal Provinces. That
was when Dr. John Robinson, Pike's former associate, again turned
up at Chihuahua, talking very suspiciously and apparently maneuvering to have Walker summoned to interpret for him. Salcedo, still incensed about Robinson's lying behavior in the Internal Provinces in
1807, used another interpreter, through whom he voiced such contempt
as to send a discouraged Robinson back to the United States in short
order. Salcedo did send a Robinson letter of 1807 to San Carlos to have
Walker certify a translation,[80] but it appears unlikely that Robinson
was able to contact Walker during that visit.

By fall, 1815, Walker was back in the field, mapping under orders
of the new commandant general of the eastern Internal Provinces, Joaquín de Arredondo. His immediate mission was to map the area from
Chihuahua to Lampazos and thence the banks of the Rio Grande to
its mouth, but he turned up at San Antonio on October 4 with a corporal and five soldiers, saying that his next commission would be to
map the province of Texas. Gov. Mariano Varela doubted that Walker
had any good reason to be in the San Antonio area and arranged for
him to continue his march that very day.[81]

Arredondo did send Walker back to Texas in December, with par

ticular orders to reconnoiter Bandera Pass. But the Texas-Coahuila frontier had grown so turbulent in the aftermath of the abortive revolution of 1813 in Texas that General Cordero could not spare enough troops
from Coahuila to escort Walker from the Rio Grande into the hills
west of San Antonio. Instead, Walker had to ride up the Camino de
la Pita from the Presidio del Rio Grande with a ten-man escort furnished him there, traveling for mutual security with the paymaster's
convoy to Béxar. En route they spotted smoke signals from a camp of
Comanche warriors. The ensuing ninety-minute skirmish was not decisive; the Comanches retired with one dead and one wounded man,
leaving one Spanish corporal and two soldiers wounded, but some lingered in the area and the poor condition of the Spaniards' horses prevented effective pursuit.[82] Prospects for mapping the hill country were
not encouraging.

Still more discouraging was the situation at San Antonio, where
Governor Varela proved no more cordial or cooperative than before.
Walker's documents from Commandant General Arredondo did not
satisfy Varela, who was awaiting Arredondo's reply to his October in-
quiry about the legitimacy of Walker's activities in Texas. Not until
the particulars arrived from Arredondo's headquarters at Monterrey
would Varela permit Walker to go on to La Bahía and other points
to continue his surveying. He even forbade Walker to take any notes
around San Antonio.[83]

Unfortunately, almost no mail was reaching or leaving Texas then
because fugitive insurrectionists were systematically disrupting communications so as to make Texas untenable for the Crown. With Indian assistance, their campaign worked so well that the commandant
general ceased to count upon mail from Texas. To forestall a complete
breakdown of communications, he ordered that events in Texas be reported from Coahuila.[84] There was virtually no chance of satisfying
Varela's conditions for the pursuit of Walker's mission.

So Juan Pedro dallied away two weeks at San Antonio, waiting
for mail that would never come, until it was nearly time to depart
with the monthly convoy to Rio Grande. The day after Christmas he
made a final appeal to the governor for permission to sketch San Antonio and the principal roads within a three- or four-mile radius. He
would need a guide familiar with the area to accompany him and the
use of a horse for a day so as to achieve at least that small part of his
assignment. He also pleaded for an account of the plots held by the
settlers and missions, the population and their crops, promising not

to report anything the governor wished omitted. Recognizing that Walker must leave with the convoy, Varela relented just enough to let a soldier assist him for a day.[85] It was a paltry outcome for Spain's last effort to map Texas.

That miserable episode of insult and frustration in Texas in 1815 provides the last firm documentary evidence, thus far, of Juan Pedro Walker's activities in this hemisphere. However, there is one more Walker map, with neither date nor title, that is thought to date from that period.

In many respects the most ambitious of all, this too is in the Huntington Library among the Berlandier papers. Like the other two of that set, it is a rough draft ($17\frac{1}{8} \times 12\frac{3}{4}$ inches) rather than a polished product. A notation, signed Juan Pedro Walker [rubric], warns of a possible distortion in longitude resulting from having drawn it hurriedly without access to the proper tables.

It runs westward from the Great Lakes and the Mississippi to the Pacific, and north to Hudson's Bay. Wheat found it to reflect a considerable amount of Mackenzie's information about the Pacific Northwest.[86] He guessed its date at 1817, reasoning that it shows information about the Missouri and Columbia rivers that could not have been available to Walker before publication of the Lewis and Clark map in 1814, but must antedate the boundary agreement of 1819. Still, it lacks details that must have appeared on the Walker map of 1810 upon which Tanner relied. Wheat would have been surprised to know that some of the details of the Missouri River which he thought could have come only from the Lewis and Clark map of 1814 actually appeared on the Walker map of 1805–1808 that we now know only from the 1969 photocopy.

Certainly this ambitious map is puzzling. So is the rest of Juan Pedro's story. In Mexico, where he is remembered only as an insurgent against Spanish rule, it is thought that Walker died shortly after independence.[87]

How astonishing, then, to find Juan Pedro in Spain five years later, petitioning the king for permission to go to New Orleans to reclaim properties that he had there. In August, 1826, at Valladolid, Walker presented himself as an unfortunate military man who had sacrificed everything in the Royal Service. He called himself the lieutenant governor of the Internal Provinces of New Spain, a startling exaggeration.[88] As usual, Juan Pedro's papers were not quite in order; he had found an influential friend to help him reach Ferdinand VII, in whose possible kindness now lay his only hope. The trail of evidence ends there, at least for the moment. What a miserable predicament in which to leave such a versatile and enterprising mapmaker.

But consider the legacy of Juan Pedro's odyssey from the swamps of the Deep South to the craggy heights of the Chihuahuan desert to the Gulf of California. The maps that he made at Chihuahua embodied the knowledge of western America that Spanish enterprise had won by the final decade of empire in New Spain. Despite their woeful attrition, his maps remain a unique record, holding more than a few correctives for the pervasive and pernicious myth of Spanish fecklessness on the northern frontier. Moreover, the record of Walker's fieldwork attests the beginning of scientific mapping in the trans-Mississippi West, and specifically in Texas, decades before the United States Army's Corps of Topographical Engineers began the process anew.[89]

In many ways Walker's is a tragic tale of bright promise too often thwarted. It dramatizes the opportunities and the dilemmas created by the collision of Anglo- and Hispanic-American frontiers. To know Juan Pedro Walker and his associates is to gain new insights into life in the lower Mississippi valley and Spain's northern frontier provinces in the dawn of the nineteenth century.

NOTES

1. Henry Schenck Tanner, "Geographical Memoir," in *New American Atlas* (Philadelphia, 1823).

2. John Hamilton Robinson, "A Map of Mexico, Louisiana, and the Missouri Territory" (Philadelphia, 1819), appears with accompanying analysis in James C. Martin and Robert Sidney Martin, *Maps of Texas and the Southwest, 1513–1900* (Albuquerque: University of New Mexico Press, 1984), pp. 116–17.

3. Andrew Ellicott to Sarah Ellicott, Camp Bayou Sarah, June 19, 1798, Papers of Andrew Ellicott, Manuscripts Division, Library of Congress (hereafter cited as Ellicott Papers), reel 2, v. 4; Donald Jackson, ed., *The Journals of Zebulon Montgomery Pike* (Norman: University of Oklahoma Press, 1966), I, 413.

4. Ellicott Papers, reel 1.

5. Professors Charles W. Harris, Samuel Holmes, and W. L. Richards, Certification of David Gillespie, University of North Carolina, September 22, 1796, Ellicott Papers, reel 2, v. 7.

6. Ellicott to Manuel Gayoso, Clarksville, April 22, 1798, Ellicott Papers, reel 1, v. 3.

7. Ellicott to Gayoso de Lemos, Natchez, July 28, 1797, Ellicott Papers, reel 1, v. 3.

8. Ellicott to Isaac Guion, Camp, June 27, 1798, and Ellicott to Secretary of State, Camp Big Bayou Sarah, June 19, 1798, Ellicott Papers, reel 1, v. 3.

9. Ellicott to Secretary of State, Camp Big Bayou Sarah, July 29, 1798, Ellicott Papers, reel 1, v. 3.

10. Ellicott to Thomas Freeman and Ellicott to Messrs. Charles Anderson, Dennis Collins, George Robbins, Andrew A. Ellicott, and John Walker, Camp, October 18, 1798; Ellicott to Winthrop Sargent, Camp, October 20, 1798, both in Ellicott Papers, reel 1, v. 3.

11. Ellicott to Secretary of State, Camp Big Bayou Sarah, July 29, 1798, Ellicott Papers, reel 1, v. 3; Ellicott to Sarah Ellicott, Camp Bayou Sarah, June 9, 1798, and Darling's Creek, November 6, 1798, Ellicott Papers, reel 2, v. 4.

12. Ellicott to Secretary of State, New Orleans, January 10, 1799, Ellicott Papers, reel 1, v. 3.

13. David Gillespie to Ellicott, Camp Mobile River, April 9, 1799, Ellicott Papers, reel 1, v. 2.

14. Ellicott to Col. Benjamin Hawkins, St. Marys, April 22, 1800, Ellicott Papers, reel 2, v. 4.

15. Ellicott to Secretary of State, Cumberland Island, March 23, 1800, Ellicott Papers, reel 2, v. 4.

16. Ellicott to Sarah Ellicott, Cumberland, April 15, 1800, Ellicott Papers, reel 2, v. 4.

17. John Walker to Gillespie, Philadelphia, July 6, 1800, Ellicott Papers, reel 2, v. 7.

18. John Walker to "Dear Father," Philadelphia, September 27, 1800, William J. Minor Papers, Louisiana State University Special Collections, Baton Rouge. The author gratefully acknowledges the courtesy of Sir Jack D. L. Holmes in informing her of this document.

19. Ellicott to Thomas Jefferson, Philadelphia, May 28 and September 17, 1800, Ellicott Papers, reel 2, v. 5.

20. Ellicott to Sarah Ellicott, Philadelphia, January 29, 1801, Ellicott Papers, reel 2, v. 5.

21. Ellicott to Robert Patterson, vice-president of the American Philosophical Society, Philadelphia, September 23, 1800, in Andrew Ellicott, *The Journal of Andrew Ellicott, Late Commissioner on behalf of the United States . . . for Determining the Boundary between the United States and the Possessions of His Catholic Majesty* (Philadelphia, 1803; reprint, Chicago: Quadrangle Books, 1962), app., pp. 43–44.

22. Ellicott to Jefferson, Philadelphia, May 13 and June 6, 1801, Ellicott Papers, reel 2, v. 5.

23. Ellicott to Jefferson, Lancaster, October 10, 1801, Ellicott Papers, reel 2, v. 5.

24. Ellicott to Jefferson, November 2, 1801, and Ellicott to Albert Gallatin, Lancaster, December 31, 1801, Ellicott Papers, reel 2, v. 5.

25. Albert Gallatin to Martin Van Buren, New York, February 18, 1830, National Archives, Record Group 76, Washington, D.C.

26. Ellicott to Winthrop Sargent, Philadelphia, August 30, 1801, and Ellicott to James Madison, Lancaster, December 29, 1801, Ellicott Papers, reel 2, v. 5; William C. C. Claiborne to Peter Walker, September 9 and 13, 1802, in Dunbar Rowland, ed., *Mississippi Territorial Archives: Letter Books of W. C. C. Claiborne* (Jackson: Mississippi Department of Archives and History, 1917), I, 168–69, 180.

27. Dunbar to Ellicott, Natchez, October 3, 1801, Ellicott Papers, reel 2, v. 5.

28. Juan Pedro Walker, three surveys (lands of Estevan Minor, William Kenner,

and Juan Minor), Concordia, September 3, 1802, in The Historic New Orleans Collection, New Orleans.

29. José Joaquín Ugarte, Census of Foreigners in Nacogdoches, January 1, 1804, Béxar Archives, Barker Texas History Center, University of Texas at Austin (hereafter cited as BA).

30. Nemesio Salcedo to Governor of Texas, Chihuahua, December 21, 1802, BA.

31. Miguel Músquiz and José María Guadiana, Diary of events in March, Nacogdoches, March 31, 1803, BA.

32. Músquiz and Guadiana, Diary of events in April, Nacogdoches, April 30, 1803; Músquiz to Juan Bautista de Elguezábal, Nacogdoches, May 6 and July 2, 1803, BA.

33. The five workmen were recorded as Jesse Smith, Miguel Richare, Guillermo Brown, Domingo Morales, and Juan Fray; Músquiz and Guadiana, Diary of events in May, Nacogdoches, May 31, 1803, and Diary of events in June, Nacogdoches, June 30, 1803, both in BA.

34. Salcedo to Elguezábal, Chihuahua, June, 1803; Músquiz to Elguezábal, Nacogdoches, July 2, 1803, both in BA.

35. Músquiz to Elguezábal, Nacogdoches, August 30, 1803, Nacogdoches Archives, Texas State Archives, Texas State Library, Austin.

36. José Joaquín Ugarte to Elguezábal, Nacogdoches, September 2, 1803, BA.

37. Salcedo to Governor of Texas, Chihuahua, October 10, 1803, BA.

38. Vidal to Ugarte, Concordia, October 4, 1803, BA (author's translation).

39. Vidal to Ugarte, Concordia, October 4, 1803, BA; Ugarte to Elguezábal, Nacogdoches, October 21, 1803, Nacogdoches Archives. Permission for the removal of Vidal's property to Nacogdoches was granted promptly, although the grant of land was delayed pending a policy decision (Salcedo to Elguezábal, Chihuahua, November 10, 1803, BA).

40. Músquiz and Guadiana, Diary of events in April, Nacogdoches, April 30, 1803; also, Diary of events in June, Nacogdoches, June 30, 1803, BA.

41. Fr. Marion A. Habig, A Biographical Dictionary, in The Zacatecan Missionaries in Texas, 1716–1834 (Austin: Texas Historical Survey Committee, 1973), pp. 139–40.

42. Elguezábal to Salcedo, Béxar, August 17, 1803; Salcedo to Elguezábal, Chihuahua, September 12, 1803. BA.

43. Fr. José María Puelles to Elguezábal, Nacogdoches, November 1, 1803 (copy of original sent to the commandant general on October 23), BA.

44. Puelles to Elguezábal, Nacogdoches, November 30, 1803 (copy of original sent to commandant general on January 4, 1804); Salcedo to Elguezábal, Chihuahua, December 12, 1803, both in BA.

45. Ugarte to Elguezábal, Nacogdoches, November 1, 1803; Puelles to Elguezábal, Nacogdoches, November 30, 1803, both in BA.

46. Juan Pedro Walker's service record for this period is drawn from the Historical Archives, Manuscripts, and Documents of Janos, microfilm in the Special Collections, Library of the University of Texas at El Paso (UTEP), reel 15; and in the Janos Collection, Benson Latin American Collection, University of Texas at Austin, folder 18. His formal service record (hoja de servicio) is missing.

47. Edward D. Turner to W. C. C. Claiborne, Fort Claiborne, December 27, 1804, in Letter Books of W. C. C. Claiborne, III, 31.

48. Salcedo to José Antonio Caballero, Chihuahua, February 5, 1805, Walker file, Archivo General Militar, Segovia.

49. Janos microfilm, reel 16, UTEP.

50. Salcedo to Cordero, Chihuahua, August 24, 1806, BA; Benedict Leutenegger, trans., and Marion A. Habig, ed., "Puelles' Report of 1827 on the Texas-Louisiana Boundary," *Louisiana History* 19 (Spring, 1978): 141-44.

51. Salcedo to Casa Calvo, Chihuahua, October 8, 1805, BA.

52. Sebastian Rodríguez to Cordero, Nacogdoches, March 4, 1806, BA. Juan Pedro appears in the document as "VVaker," one of several variants which the name Walker suffers in Spanish orthography.

53. Rodríguez to Cordero, Nacogdoches, March 19, 1806, BA.

54. Salcedo to Cordero, Chihuahua, June 16, 1806, Lamar Papers, Document 2875, Texas State Archives.

55. The fullest treatment of the Freeman expedition appears in Dan L. Flores, ed., *Jefferson and Southwestern Exploration: The Freeman and Custis Accounts of the Red River Expedition of 1806* (Norman: University of Oklahoma Press, 1984). Unfortunately, a misreading of evidence has led Flores to misconstrue Juan Pedro Walker's family history and also to the erroneous conclusion that Juan Pedro Walker ascended the Red River in 1804 (pp. 40-42).

56. Dunbar to Jefferson, Natchez, May 13, 1804, and Jefferson to Dunbar, April 16, 1806, in Eron Rowland Dunbar, ed., *The Life, Letters and Papers of William Dunbar* (Jackson: Press of the Mississippi Historical Society, 1930), p. 131.

57. Salcedo to Cordero, Chihuahua, August 14 and October 2, 1806, BA.

58. Fr. José María Puelles, Mapa de la Provincia de Texas, 180[torn]. MS in the Barker Texas History Center, Austin. While this is cataloged as an 1807 map, it is equally plausible to assume that Puelles drew it in 1806.

59. Freeman's Journal as redacted by Nicholas King, in Flores, ed., *Jefferson and Southwestern Exploration*, pp. 204-205.

60. Salcedo to Cordero, Chihuahua, August 24, 1806; Dionisio Valle, Monthly Report, Nacogdoches, August 31, 1806, both in BA.

61. Dionisio Valle to Commandant of Orcoquisac, Nacogdoches, October 22, 1806, BA.

62. Viana to Cordero, Nacogdoches, May 1, 1807; Cordero to Viana, Béxar, May 16, 1807, BA.

63. General Wilkinson was a friend of Peter Walker, in whose care he left the ailing Mrs. Wilkinson at Natchez in 1799 when he hurried to report to President Jefferson, and subsequently (Wilkinson to Ellicott, New Orleans, June 12, 1799, Ellicott Papers, reel 1, v. 2). Wilkinson had surely encountered Juan Pedro on the general's visits to Ellicott's survey camp, and perhaps their paths crossed in Washington, too. Colonel Cushing carried young John Walker's letter and gifts to Peter Walker from Philadelphia in 1800.

64. Salcedo to Governor of Texas, Chihuahua, March 11, 1809, BA.

65. Jackson, ed., *Journals of Pike*, I, 413-22; and II, 64, 67, 147, 178, provides more information about Walker than any other published source.

66. Walker's transcripts of the Pike documents are in the Archivo Histórico Nacional, Madrid, in Estado, Legajo 5548, expediente 20, and Legajo 5557, expediente 10.

67. For analyses of the Pike and Robinson maps, see Martin and Martin, *Maps of Texas and the Southwest*, pp. 111, 117.

68. Carl I. Wheat, *Mapping the Trans-Mississippi West* (San Francisco: The Institute of Historical Cartography, 1958), I, 251; II, 205.

69. C. H. Muller, introduction to Jean Louis Berlandier, *Journey to Mexico during the Years 1826 to 1834* (Austin: Texas State Historical Association, 1980), I, xi.

70. Wheat, *Mapping the Trans-Mississippi West*, I, 251; II, 205.

71. Gonzalo López de Haro to Juan Jabat, México, November 12, 1808, Papeles de Estado 58E, Document 97 (v. 82–117): "Plano y noticias que entragó en México el teniente de frigata don Gonzalo López de Haro al comisionado don Juan Jabat, a peticion de este, como encargado que es quel por la Corte, para formar un plano exacto de las provincias internas de México, tanto orientales como occidentales. Hacia 1808." MS Proc. Legajo 58, signatura 55, Archivo Histórico Nacional, Madrid.

72. In 1969, during the course of her research on the Spanish Royal Corps of Engineers, Dr. Janet Fireman, now of the Los Angeles County Museum of Natural History, noticed the Walker map in the Biblioteca Central Militar in Madrid and sent a photocopy to Michael Weber, a scholar of southwestern cartography who is now director of the Arizona Heritage Society. It is through his courtesy that I have a photocopy.

73. Salcedo to Casa Calvo, Chihuahua, October 8, 1805, BA.

74. Janos microfilm, reel 15, UTEP.

75. Sgt. Baltazar Acosta, paymaster of Janos Company, Distribución, Chihuahua, January 28, 1809, Janos Collection, Benson Latin American Collection.

76. Originally bound in *Histórica*, v. 542, f. 235bis, it is now filed as AGN mapa 450, Archivo General de la Nación, Mexico City.

77. Juan Pedro Walker, Translation of forty-six documents, Chihuahua, April 20, 1811, BA.

78. *Diccionario Porrúa de historia, biografía y geografía de México*, 3rd ed., 2 vols. (Mexico City: Editorial Porrúa, S.A., 1971), II, 2292.

79. José María Miguel i Vergés, *Diccionario de insurgentes* (Mexico: Editorial Porrúa, S.A., 1969), p. 613.

80. Juan Pedro Walquer, Certification of translation of Robinson to Salcedo, Chihuahua, April 23, 1807, signed at San Carlos, January 18, 1813 (copied at Chihuahua, February 9, 1813, by Francisco Velasco). Archivo Histórico Nacional, Estado, Legajo 5557, f. 1015. Photocopy in Manuscripts Division, Library of Congress.

81. José Antonio Bustillos to Mariano Varela, Mission La Espada, October 4, 1815; Varela to Joaquín de Arredondo, Béxar, October 12, 1815, both in BA.

82. Walker to Varela, Béxar, December 9, 1815, BA.

83. Varela to Arredondo, Béxar, December 19, 1815; Walker to Varela, Béxar, December 26, 1815, both in BA.

84. Matías Jiménez to Varela, Rió Grande, December 9, 1815, BA.

85. Walker to Varela and Varela to Walker, December 26, 1815, BA.

86. Wheat, *Mapping the Trans-Mississippi West*, II, 64.

87. *Diccionario Porruá*, II, 2292.

88. Walker file, Archivo General Militar.

89. The story of the Corps of Topographical Engineers is told in William H. Goetzmann, *Army Exploration in the American West, 1803–1863* (New Haven, Conn.: Yale University Press, 1959).

Seeing and Believing: The Explorer and the Visualization of Place

ON A JULY DAY in 1873 a small party of explorers struggled up the bare, rocky slopes of Notch Mountain in western Colorado. As they made their way above the timberline, one of their number, the photographer William H. Jackson, climbed over the shoulder of the mountain and beheld one of nature's wonders for the first time. "I emerged above the timberline, and the clouds," he later remembered, "and suddenly, as I clambered over a vast mass of jagged rocks, I discovered . . . [a] great shining cross there before me, tilted against the mountainside." The cross was formed by snow caught in the shaded crevices of an otherwise bare mountain face tilted up to the July sun. Jackson quickly unlimbered his heavy wet-plate camera equipment and stood poised to photograph this most awe-inspiring of nature's wonders, when suddenly a rainbow arched across the sky, framing, as it were, the holy cross. Jackson took his picture even as the expedition artist, William Henry Holmes, sketched it, rainbow and all. There, deep in an unexplored part of the Rockies, the Creator had presented a sure sign of his sublime blessing of America's Manifest Destiny. The Mount of the Holy Cross, with its divine message, quickly became a famous source of inspiration to Americans, as Jackson sold copies of his photograph and dramatic stories about his great discovery were published in the newspapers.

The mountain became even more famous when Jackson's friend Thomas Moran quickly traveled to western Colorado and made a monumental, even if garishly embellished, painting of it, which was in turn reproduced as an elaborate woodcut and distributed to thousands.[1] A scientific exploring and map-making party had discovered God. Never mind that Jackson had to retouch his photograph just a bit to make both sides of the snowy crossbar stand out clearly. And never mind that Thomas Moran almost completely invented the scene in his popular painting and its various woodcut copies. Dr. Ferdinand V. Hayden and his men of the United States Geological and Geo-

William H. Jackson's sketch of himself at work with a wet plate camera on the Mountain of the Holy Cross in western Colorado (1873). (Still Photographs, National Archives, Washington, D.C.)

graphical Survey had visualized the sublime in the Rockies for all time. Science and religion were joined in the American West in the latter half of the nineteenth century.

This story illustrates the way in which scientific explorers of what I have called the "Second Great Age of Discovery"—the late eighteenth and the entire nineteenth centuries — rapidly visualized in hundreds of different ways, with thousands of different meanings, not only North America, but all of the islands, oceans, ice masses and continental interiors of the globe.[2] This was an age in which first the artist and then later the photographer were important components of any serious exploring expedition. This was the age that first really visualized the whole earth and its many exotic peoples.

The American West, that vast unknown at the beginning of the nineteenth century, provides a significant case study of the many ways in which explorers made visual interpretations that simplified the complex geography of a place or places that the masses of people could not yet experience for themselves. In providing these visual conceptions of place, artist-explorers contributed to America's story about itself — its myth — as much or more than any of its writers have done. They have also dramatized the feats of American explorers who ventured out from North America onto the oceans, the jungles and high mountains of South America, Africa, the South Seas, and the frozen ends of the earth. Thus, the views of American artist-explorers contributed uncountable images of the American as part of world culture, pursuing a divinely ordained destiny. The "Second Great Age of Discovery" was an age of belief, of faith in science, and in the empirical observer who was the antenna of the scientific community and, indeed, the whole culture.

At first, artist-explorers rendered interpretations of the West in maps. Lewis and Clark's masterful map showed the West to be a vast and complex system of rivers and mountains and curious Indian tribes. Their map was followed by a continual succession of maps, made first by military explorers such as John C. Frémont, then by cartographers on the great post–Civil War surveys, such as those led by Clarence King and Ferdinand V. Hayden, then finally by the United States Geological Survey and the ERTS satellite photomaps of NASA.

The first real artist to record the West, Samuel Seymour, who accompanied an army expedition across the Great Plains to the Rockies in 1819–20, pictured the vast plains as almost empty, save for a few buffalo and a range of towering mountains. In a work of 1819 he portrayed all this from a position fifty miles out from the front range of the Rockies. He also added a few Indian observers and the bones of some primeval beast who had perished in one of the great inundations of the continent. Seymour also painted Pike's Peak in a rainstorm, thus contradicting the expedition's leader, Maj. Stephen H. Long, who declared the plains a "Great Desert." More than that, in a seeming conspiracy with the expedition's geologist, Seymour had subtly portrayed the long evolution of the continent at a time when Europeans and Americans alike argued whether it was even the biblical 4,004 years old.[3] But most of all, in one dramatic picture of the Rockies from fifty miles out, Seymour, clumsy artist that he was, managed to portray the vast emptiness of the West.

George Catlin, on the other hand, traveling up the Missouri in 1832, saw in the vast prairies a green and pleasant land, peopled by noble savages who for the most part were uncorrupted by the white man. For him, the West was a paradise of flocks and herds and sublimely innocent people, all of which was about to be lost. Catlin's West was the first of the eyewitness Edenic visions of that half of the continent, though his West was not without the dangers of the buffalo charge, the terrors of the sweeping prairie fires, and the secret torture rituals of a lost tribe of "Welsh" Indians, the Mandans.[4]

Following close on the heels of Catlin, Prince Maximilian of Wied Neu-Wied on the Rhine, made the trip up the Missouri with his own artist, Karl Bodmer.[5] In 1833–34 Bodmer interpreted not only the West, but America, with his hauntingly beautiful watercolors. No one ever painted the American Indian as well as Bodmer, but in some ways his landscapes are even more startling. The prince expected America to be a primitive country overrun with jungles. Bodmer painted civilization penetrating the wilderness all the way to the Mississippi, and then he became fascinated with the steamboat culture on the Ohio and Mississippi rivers. He was a visual gazetteer in recording the rapid advance of Americans through the forests of the Ohio country, and across the plains of Indiana and Illinois, but he was at his best in visualizing the upper Missouri country of the Mandan, Assiniboin, Sioux, and Blackfoot. Here he painted vast panoramas that portrayed hundreds of miles of prairie country. He painted distant views of the Rockies. He caught exactly the weird sandstone formations that looked like fairytale castles along the upper Missouri. And he painted the freezing Dakota winter settling over the immense plains as no one has before or since. Bodmer saw America as a vast and varied country, which he rendered as one of extraordinary beauty.

In the summer of 1837 the young Baltimore artist Alfred Jacob Miller went west with a Scottish baronet and a band of mountain men.[6] Besides being the only artist ever to record the mountain men firsthand, Miller also visualized the West as a deeply romantic place. Partly influenced by Thomas Cole's gentle rendering of the Catskills and partly by the English romantic painter J. M. W. Turner, Alfred Jacob Miller portrayed the West as a mountainous, pastoral Eden. He painted high mountain lakes in the moonlight, Indians bathing in flowing mountain streams as innocently as any South Sea native, and long hidden valleys or "holes" where the mountain men trapped, rendezvoused, or ran for their lives from hostile Indians.

In general these early artist-explorers viewed the West as a vast, pristine paradise. Later artists accompanying exploring parties went even further in this direction. In the 1860s, as the country was being torn apart by Civil War, a war photographed in all its horrors by Mathew Brady's photographers, Albert Bierstadt painted gigantic canvases of the heart of the Rockies and a bit later, Yosemite. When on display, his large Wagnerian canvases not only distracted people from the war for a moment, they also represented a nationalistic anthem to America itself.[7] In addition, with his Wagnerian effects portrayed in remote towering mountains, fabled inland lakes, clouds that represent both glory and *Sturm und Drang*, and the enormous ice-age room that was Yosemite, Bierstadt began the designation of places in the West that became "sacred spaces." He was followed in this process by Dr. Hayden's painter, Thomas Moran, who became as famous for his stunningly beautiful, even grand paintings of Yellowstone and the Grand Canyon, as he was for his portrayal of the Mount of the Holy Cross. The places Bierstadt and Moran chose to paint as "sacred spaces" —Yosemite, Yellowstone, and the Grand Canyon—were eventually recognized by the Congress of the United States as such, and were set aside as the first national wilderness parks in the world.[8] The West was a polychrome wonderland.

Other artist-explorers, especially those connected with the surveying and building of transcontinental railroads, whether painters or photographers, represented the West as the scene of progress. The West was the setting for the inevitable spread of Anglo-Saxon mechanized civilization around the globe, as foretold by that mighty founder of the geographical sciences, the Prussian explorer Alexander von Humboldt, whose titanic visions dominated the first half of the nineteenth century. In line with this, military artists painted or sketched or mapped routes for the railroads. Others portrayed the Oregon and California trails in visual, highly speculative roadmap pictures. Few dwelt upon barren places, like the Mojave Desert, as did Lt. George Brewerton. Instead, artists like John Mix Stanley recorded endless herds of buffalo on the Dakota prairies, incredibly beautiful spots along the Columbia River, and even in the Gila River country of the far Southwest, amazingly beautiful ecological collages that wished away the deserts and the Apache in favor of dazzling displays of plant and animal life.[9] A whole generation of artist-explorers intent upon stimulating settlement and progress viewed the West, especially Oregon and California, as "the promised land." None did this better than William Jewett, whose most famous work pictured the American River, scene of the great gold strike in 1848, as a pastoral paradise. One of his works, done in 1850, was appropriately titled *The Promised Land*. These "booster" artists echoed the patriotic sentiments of explorers such as Lt. John C. Frémont, who symbolically waved a homemade eagle flag atop what he thought was the highest peak overlooking the trail to California. In official government reports that were really national anthems, he bade the people—young men, old men, women, children, and even Mormons —to go West.[10] Frémont thought he was one of those gods rhetorically placed atop the Rocky Mountains by his jingoistic father-in-law, Sen. Thomas Hart Benton of Missouri. As much as possible, Frémont made himself the embodiment of Manifest Destiny.

Other artist-explorers of the time, tramping through the Southwest, stumbled upon the hidden lost citadels of the vanished Anasazi civilization. Artists, such as Richard Kern, in painting such places as the Canyon de Chelly and the immense, deserted pueblos of Chaco Canyon, placed before the world the Luxors and Abu Simbels of America.[11] They added more than a touch of mystery and exoticism to the West. Even Thomas Moran, in a later period, contributed to the spirit of the mysterious West with his strange painting, *The Spirit of the Indian*, portraying a gigantic seated figure carved out of the Rockies in a preview of another "sacred" place, Mount Rushmore in the Black Hills of South Dakota.[12]

And, as if to add to those images of progress created by railroad scouts, as well as Currier & Ives' Fanny Palmer, whose *Across the Continent* was an icon to millions, there were still other artists of a more profound bent who saw the West in its natural state as part of a process that over millennia was shaping the earth. Perhaps no one matched William H. Holmes in this respect. His drawings and paintings of the Grand Canyon and the whole uplifted Colorado Plateau created a visual model for what was happening someplace, somewhere on the earth, at whatever time one cared to name. The West was for Holmes not a place, not even a sacred space, but a vision of nature's processes. It was a giant, natural engineering marvel.[13]

Thus, the West provided many kinds of visualizations of place for American and foreign artist-explorers. To recapitulate, the West was variously a great prairie Eden, a paradise of noble red men as well as flocks and herds. It was a promised land, the setting for the greatest progress and prosperity of all times in history. It was mountains in the moonlight, vast sweeping, endless horizons, hidden places of mystery and lost civilizations suggesting a past more ancient than that of Europe; it was the scene of grandeur and of spectacular sacred places "commensurate with man's capacity for wonder." But, above all, for the artist-explorers, it was the scene of that "high adventure" about which Walter Webb wrote so eloquently in his presidential address to the American Historical Association. Quite possibly, for our time, the art historian Barbara Novak has correctly characterized the spirit and achievement of the artist-explorers of the American West. She has written: "In Europe the tour de force generally received its scale from the artist's ambition set resplendently within a major tradition; in America it consisted of simply 'getting there.' The artist became the hero of his own journey — by vanquishing the physical obstacles en route to a destination. For the ambition of the artistic enterprise was substituted the ambition of the artist's Quest — itself a major nineteenth century theme."[14]

It is in their quests, out of which came the multiple visions of the American West, that the artist-explorers, good and bad by European standards, helped to create the fundamental myth or story of America. From their struggles up rivers, over mountains, across deserts, and out of their imaginations, stunned by the terrifying beauties of such wonders as Yosemite, Yellowstone, and the "grandest canyon of them all," came that highly illustrated "brag skin" that is the tale of our tribe. And that tale is a fundamental part of the Second Great Age of Discovery, a profound world-event that has shaped all our lives.

NOTES

1. See William H. Goetzmann, *Exploration and Empire* (New York: Alfred A. Knopf, 1966), p. 228. Also see Thurman Wilkins, *Thomas Moran, Artist of the Mountains* (Norman: University of Oklahoma Press, 1966), pp. 101–103.

2. See William H. Goetzmann, *New Lands, New Men: America and the Second Great Age of Discovery* (New York: Viking Press, 1986), especially the picture portfolios. Also see, for example, Herman Viola and Caroline Margolis, *Magnificent Voyagers* (Washington: Smithsonian Institution Press, 1986) that features the Great United States Exploring Expedition that sailed around the world in the years 1838–42.

3. See Seymour's painting, frontispiece to Edwin James, *Account of an Expedition from Pittsburg to the Rocky Mountains Performed in the Years 1819, '20 . . .* (Philadelphia: H. C. Carey and I. Lea, Chestnut Street, 1823). Also see its appendix on geology.

4. George Catlin, *Letters and Notes on the Manners, Customs, and Conditions*

of North America Indians (London, 1844), Letter no. 22, I, 155–84. Also see Catlin, *O-Kee-Pa, A Religious Ceremony and Other Customs of the Mandan*, ed. John Ewers (New Haven, Conn.: Yale University Press, 1967), *passim*.

5. See William H. Goetzmann and William Orr, *Karl Bodmer's America* (Lincoln and London: University of Nebraska Press and Joslyn Art Museum, 1984). This is the definitive work on Bodmer and the discussion that follows is based upon it and the Maximilian of Wied Neu-Wied papers at the Joslyn Art Museum.

6. See Ron Tyler, ed., *Alfred Jacob Miller: Artist on the Oregon Trail* (Fort Worth: Amon Carter Museum, 1982). Also see Marvin C. Ross, *The West of Alfred Jacob Miller*, rev. ed. (Norman: University of Oklahoma Press, 1968).

7. See Nancy Anderson, "Albert Bierstadt and California," Ph.D. diss., University of Delaware, 1986. This is by far the best work to date on Bierstadt.

8. Alfred Runte, *National Parks: The American Experience* (Lincoln and London: University of Nebraska Press, 1979, 1981).

9. See William H. Goetzmann and William N. Goetzmann, *The West of the Imagination* (London and New York: W. W. Norton, 1986).

10. See William H. Goetzmann, *Army Exploration in the American West, 1803–1863* (New Haven, Conn.: Yale University Press, 1959), pp. 82–84.

11. See David J. Weber, *Richard H. Kern, Expeditionary Artist in the Far Southwest, 1848–1853* (Albuquerque: University of New Mexico Press, 1985).

12. This strange Moran painting is owned by the Philbrook Art Center in Tulsa, Oklahoma.

13. William H. Goetzmann, *William H. Holmes, Panoramic Artist* (Fort Worth: Amon Carter Museum, 1977).

14. Barbara Novak, *Nature and Culture: American Landscape and Painting, 1825–1875* (New York: Oxford University Press, 1980), p. 137.